CONCILIUM

D1528857

CONCILIUM 2000/2

CREATING IDENTITY

Edited by
Hermann Häring, Maureen Junker-Kenny
and Dietmar Mieth

SCM Press · London

Published by SCM Press, 9–17 St Albans Place,
London N1

Copyright © Stichting Concilium

English translations © 2000 SCM–Canterbury Press Ltd

ISBN: 0 334 03058 7

Typeset by Regent Typesetting, London
Printed by Biddles, Ltd, Guildford and King's Lynn

Concilium Published February, April, June, October,
December.

Contents

Introduction

Identity – Biographical, Moral, Religious

In this issue of *Concilium* we attempt to document the thematic, interdisciplinary work which characterizes the new face of this theological journal. The editors and contributions represent a series of theological disciplines in which the theme of 'Identity', as discussed in the following reflections, has become important.

The question of a good life which is determined by persons themselves is central to the context of individualization. Today this determination no longer follows a tendency from outside inwards, i.e. by identification with religious and social institutions, but comes about through reassuring oneself of one's own identity, by involvement in a biography. Thus the identity of the moral and religious subject is formed by way of narrative.

Here as far as possible an original or 'authentic' form of life is sought. This question is reconstructed in philosophical theories about the individual 'good life' (*totum bene vivere*), but it has also been criticized. The question can also be found in aesthetic literature. Other topics here are the limits of identity, obstacles towards the formation of identity and broken identity. Here also belongs cultural difference in the acceptance or contesting of the identity paradigm or in developing it. The emphasis on the individual is matched by a constant collective approach. Moreover, all symbols of a successful biography have a significance which transcends the individual. Theological discussion has long been preoccupied with this problem of an identity on which claims are made and to which assignations are given, yet which remains fragile. The question of religious identity – here posed from the perspective of the question of the possibility of moral identity – has found various pointed answers: the dominance of others ('the face of the other' – E. Lévinas and E. Dussel), reflection on the self, relationality and the transcendent nature of the subject. These various interpretations at the same time put the identity theorem in question. This problem is further heightened by the inhumanity with which identity is withheld, withdrawn or alienated in the case of whole groups of people. The earliest written testimonies of Christianity show how the significance of the person of Jesus was first of all expressed in confessional formulae and hymns and then in the literary form of narratives about his life and fate. The understanding of Christianity came about through the formation of narrative resources.

At all events, the question how each of us finds our own identity as agents is not only relevant to ethics, but in the last resort also determines the question of our own religious identity. 'Identity – biographical, moral, religious' is an attempt to demonstrate social and religious developments and make them conceptually understandable by means of philosophical and theological considerations.

The theme is also important for social ethics and the theory of institutions: in what conditions can there be rightly talk of a distinctive, individual approach?

The social approach to these questions (Part I) is opened up with a look at literature (D. Mieth), Milan Kundera's novel *Identity*. This is above all about opportunities and dangers for identity in a relationship of love. A. W. Musschenga analyses the process of the formation of identity in a so-called 'individualized' society. He draws attention above all to the break with closed solid identities and the fragmentary character of personal identity. As a counter-move to the European-American debate Felix Wilfred refers to the manifold loss of identity in the two-thirds world, the intervention in personal, social and cultural identities. A. Kleinfeld discusses the economic and ethical aspect of identity among the global players and shows its positive aspects.

Two important theoreticians of identity are treated in the philosophical-ethical discussion: Charles Taylor by Thomas Gil and Paul Ricoeur by Hille Haker. This clarifies the critical debate on the model of authenticity, which ties identity to individual originality and overlooks its industrial fabrication, and also both the debate on individual atomism in the liberal theory of contract and the relationship between narrative, biographical and moral identity. Jim Keenan discusses identity as the visionary goal of the classical doctrine of virtues. Luiz C. Susin introduces contemporary debate on the limits of the philosophical model of identity which in the history of Western culture hindered the development of the other.

The theological discussion leads from the formation of Christian identity through narrative (A. del Aqua) to the history of Jesus, in which this identity finds its beginning and its end (Hermann Häring). Christine Firer-

Hinze emphasizes the experience of difference in feminist theology, the discussion of power and marginalization. Here identity appears as solidarity reflected on. In conclusion Hans G. Ulrich takes up the element of process in becoming a self, to which are added on the one hand a particular vulnerability from the origin of faith and on the other hand critical power.

In these contributions identity does not have the connotation of a claimed place of refuge but corresponds to a search for assurance under a constant threat and questioning by force from without and danger from within. Thus behind every piece of specialist information stands the ever-relevant question of the unity of biographical, moral and religious authority.

Hermann Häring, Maureen Junker-Kenny and Dietmar Mieth

I. Approaches

Moral Identity – How is it Narrated?

DIETMAR MIETH

A paradigm of the question of identity: Milan Kundera's novel *Identity**

The external course of the story which Kundera tells is easy to relate. Chantal, who has lost a five-year-old son and subsequently has been abandoned by her husband, lives with Jean-Marc, who is five years younger than she is. The very intensive symbiosis, in the 'midst' of which she stands as the real wage-earner, while he leads a marginal existence, is subjected to a test when the couple are separated for a night. Chantal also sees herself separated from her beloved's gaze – the metaphor of the gaze, the eye and the blink play a great role – and therefore for the first time she feels alone again. So she falls back into her prehistory in which under the metaphor 'rose fragrance' she saw herself as a body desired by many. Now, in a kind of early midlife crisis, expressed physically in flushes which are associated with her tendency to blush when making love, she finds that 'men no longer turn round to look at her' (13). Obviously being desired becomes a thermometer, if she interprets herself in terms of her separated self and not the loving other. This experience of the world distances her from Jean-Marc, who in his concern thinks that he has to offer her the fulfilment of this promiscuous longing and to play a fictitious admirer under the cipher CdB (Cyrano de Bergerac), the ghost writer. She joins in the game of fantasy, but this isolates her even further from Jean-Marc, from whom she must conceal what is open to him. When she finally sees through his game he appears an informer, a spy and a manipulator, who violates her rights and her intimacy. The danger of indifference which begins with this violation, that in this way both existences will be handed over to the world of conventions, appearance and meaning-lessness (descriptions of the function of erotic advertising in films and dreamed-of sex parties), results in a dream about separation and a vain search, or rather a nightmare. However, the author grants this a final awakening (152f.), in which the need for a constant gaze (without blinking, the metaphor for fluttering the eyelashes and winking) is confirmed. Thus it is finally left open whether this is more a dismantling of love or a plea for love.

Why is the story called *Identity*? At one point there is a first indication: 'Child: an existence without a biography . . . She stood guard over his irreplaceable individuality' (29). As the child is already dead, it becomes clear that this cannot be humanly possible. There is much speculation about death and life – including the catechism question 'Why are we here below? Why are we living?' (129), with a tendency towards cynicism. The answer is that we live between an insignificance celebrated with euphoria and an inability to achieve consistent and continual meaning. So Chantal alternates between two or three faces, between her erotic physicality, her professional coldness and seriousness and her security in love. By contrast Jean-Marc, as long as love dominates, is her leader and seducer; outside this sphere there is only failed 'marginal existence' (broken-off study, etc). Identity in love is based on continuity in the incomparability of the beloved (20). In this story love and identity are in a dangerous and endangered reciprocal relationship. Love gives identity because it offers the different identities ('faces') an ordered unity. Love as 'concern' endangers identity. Love rescues from the danger of the levelling down of the other; as we shall see, it works as a 'contract' against the banality of the body as a 'secretion machine' and against the conventional flatness of antiquated contexts ('clan') and the modern instrumentalization of eroticism in terms of transitory attraction.

Only after a good third of the book does the word 'identity' from the title appear, under the metaphor of the eye, which has already been mentioned:

> The eye, the window to the soul; the centre of the face's beauty; the point where a person's identity is concentrated; but at the same time an optical instrument that requires constant washing, wetting, maintenance by a special liquid dosed with salt. So the gaze, the greatest marvel man possesses, is regularly interrupted by a mechanical washing action. Like a windscreen washed by a wiper (58f.).

Kundera pursues the dualism thus addressed between the 'metaphor' as a way in which bodily expression points beyond itself on the one hand and on the other hand the actual physical nature which we overlook, indeed forget, with its moisture and its exclusions, into his figures. Chantal feels 'disgust' and 'abhorrence' at spit and wet kisses; but she is as it were changed from her body outwards in her metaphorical identity, whether as an erotic adventuress (metaphor rose fragrance) or as a beloved reflected in the gaze of the lover, or as a serious professional woman who ends up in conventionality. It is the same with Jean-Marc: 'he saw the windscreen-wiper of Chantal's eyelid as her soul's wing, a wing that trembled, that panicked, that fluttered' (61).

Jean-Marc has no professional face, no professional 'identity'; he has these, like the 'baby-tree men' whom Chantal mocks (they carry the children on their backs, on their fronts, lead them by the hand, alongside their wives), in the staging of love. When this fails, he falls back to the periphery, comes close to the poor and the beggars, while his woman remains 'in the midst' of conventional existences.

The danger of a discontinuity and a loss of consistency in relationships lies on the one hand in an 'indifference' and 'speechlessness' which grows with time. There is constant talk, indeed philosophizing, about 'boredom' and 'indifference'. On the other hand there is the danger of adapting to the norms of a culture of attraction, of which the professional, in the person of the advertising director Leroy, a Trotskyite who is 'sharp as a scalpel', says, 'The issue is to find the images that keep up the erotic appeal without intensifying the frustrations' (49). Jean-Marc tries the latter for Chantal. But the 'key experiment' with which he wants to reinforce her self-acceptance at the same time presents itself as abuse and generates in her only a reaction of indifference towards him. Conversely, he thinks that by strengthening her in an erotic sense of self, which in her view lies on the level of conventionality, he has 'changed her in her identity' (cf. 81). And when Chantal goes in search of the identity of the man who secretly writes her admiring letters, already strongly suspecting that it is Jean-Marc himself, the graphologist she asks refuses to confirm the 'identity' because he regards this as 'denunciation' (93).

The effects on the lover are described: 'His jealousy was not the same sort as he had known in his youth when his imagination would set off some agonizing erotic fantasy; this was less painful but more destructive: very gradually, it was transforming a beloved woman into the simulacrum of a beloved woman. And since she was no longer a reliable person for him, there was now no stable point in the valueless chaos which is the world. Faced with this transubstantiated (or desubstantiated) Chantal, he felt a strange melancholy apathy overtake him. Not apathy about her but apathy about everything. If Chantal is a simulacrum, then so is the whole of Jean-Marc's life' (96f.).

Where is the way out of this entanglement? If the body loses the significance that it has in love and friendship, then it can only be painted over in the style of advertising: 'We put make-up on desolation' (133). That remark us made in the catechism-chapters in 'hell' (in the dream a journey through the Channel Tunnel between France and England). Chantal also thinks there: 'Since the insignificance of all things is our lot, we should not bear it as an affliction but learn how to enjoy it' (134).

The hell of insignificance already conjured up by Albert Camus is not godless, but cynical chatter to God: 'Why are we living? To provide God with human flesh' (130). As God is a Moloch, where does deliverance lie? Lovers are asked absolutely to guarantee their identity, indeed to maintain their identity in stress. For deliverance there is only the *dream*, which reflects past, present and future in the mode of contemporaneity:

> What troubled her so, she thinks, is the dream's effect of nullifying the present . . . That is why she dislikes dreams: they impose an unacceptable equivalence among the various periods of the same life, a levelling contemporaneity of everything a person has ever experienced (6).

The past spreads itself in the dream and so does the future. The deliverance in the hellish dream is:

> But who can help her? In that moment of extreme anxiety, she glimpses again the image of a man struggling against the crowd to get her. Someone is twisting his arm behind his back; she cannot see his face, sees only his contorted figure. Good Lord, she wishes she could remember him a little more clearly; call up his features, but she can't manage it, she knows only that it is the man who loves her and that that's all that matters to her now (146f.).

The reader knows that Jean-Marc has dreamed this dream from the other side (cf.135). Love is the only thing that safeguards identity, just as Chantal's mother's love maintains the identity of her dead five-year-old son:

> She is naked, but they keep on stripping her! Stripping her of her self! Stripping her of her destiny! They'll give her a different name and then abandon her among strangers to whom she can never explain who she is:

. . . The beginning is her name, her real name. What she wants to achieve first, as an indispensable minimum, is to have this man call her by her name, her real name . . . The thought of the man who loved her returns to mind. If he were here, he would call her by her name . . . (150).

And so it comes about: the calling of her name breaks through her nightmare: 'It's not real,' says the beloved (152). Now comes the narrator's comment: 'And I ask myself: Who was dreaming? Who dreamed this story? Who imagined it? She? He? Both of them? Each one for the other? And starting when did their real life change into this treacherous fantasy? . . . Where is the border?' (152f.). At any rate the loves learn from this narrative ethic that the gaze of love which can oversee, forget and look beyond corresponds to a 'contract' which God himself has imposed upon us (58). And, from the mouth of the cynic, 'man has no right to change what God has created' (127).

The philosophy (or theology) of the novel remains fluid. Kundera is playing with many implicit readers. The only thing that is clear is the theory of the gaze of love which creates and preserves identity. But it remains open whether this is humanly possible. The lover is rightly 'anxious' about the second 'when my gaze goes out' (153), for not only his but also her identity depends on the metaphor which the name for the body sketches out. And seen in the light of reality, this name is deception. But in the world of metaphors which judge people ('gaze'), it is a higher truth, the right picture as opposed to many false pictures: the right identity

II. The message of form

Narrative ethics in literature are disclosed by the form. The 'exciting what?' of the motif narrated must retreat behind the 'how'. Certainly the form can also be secondary to the shaping, if the novelist uses it only as a vehicle for a philosophy. But in that case the narration would only be illustration, just as pictures can serve as illustrations. Once one has the content, one can change and vary the form. But if the form is binding on the content in such a way that the content can appear fully only in the form, then we must retell the story if we want to grasp the intention which is typical of it.

At least three formal characteristics are decisive for Kundera's narrative. There is the artifice which gives an everyday situation such a turn that it becomes threatening: there is the hovering between dream world and reality, in which the dream takes on a twofold function, of disturbing and delivering; and there is the artifice with the experiment in love in which the

lover appears as his rival, at the same time a literary reminiscence and a vari-
ation on Cyrano de Bergerac. Form loves oppositions and prefers a dialectic
which is not done away with in a synthesis. Thus what is serious can be
addressed only in an ironic and cynical tone; conversely, what is apparently
light and playful takes on a significant weight. However, persons retain
their individual profile, and do not simply rigidify into types, pawns on the
dialectical field. The hovering between dream and reality is matched by the
hovering between body and gaze. The gaze selects the body for a specific
perception which no longer sees the whole extension of flat reality, but only
brings together particular features. Thus the gaze has a metaphorical effect:
it puts together signs from the other which it draws on as meanings from the
multiplicity of the whole.

Although the composition of the narrative is highly artificial, the individual events which are narrated in the chapters do work, above all through
the artistic interlocking of the motifs, to shape of the scene, like 'natural'
events which are taken for granted. But perception of them always takes
place through a subject – alternating between the two lovers. Thus Chantal
sees families at leisure and on the playgrounds by the sea within the horizon
of where she is ('Why don't men turn round to look at me any longer?'). The
fathers who have baby-trees seem to her inadequate to fulfil her need, but
really it is the other way round: where she is makes her perceive the men as
people with other interests.

There is also a play on deception in the perception of the other person.
When Jean-Marc is looking for Chantal on the shore, for a long time he
mistakes another woman for her. This possibility of optical deception over
bodily identity can also seem to be a lack of knowledge and can be interpreted in that way: thus Chantal does not recognize the man (Jean-Marc)
who wants to press through to her in the crowd, and she does not know that
in feeling this longing at the same time she is desiring her beloved.

But deception does not serve merely to refer to a disappointment in love.
Rather, in the positive sense it is constitutive of the look in relationship
which makes a choice. The silence about public circumstances, the cautious
treatment of dependencies, all that corresponds to the selective perception
necessary for identity which cannot be dissolved into a sum of individual
parts capable of analysis. Identity is truth as literary expression, not truth as
the depiction of realities. Identity is a concentration of character, not an
addition of personal characteristics.

III. The philosophy of friendship and Platonic love

A sub-theme of identity, over and above the relationship of the couple, is friendship. First of all a failed friendship, between Jean-Marc and F, serves as paradigm. The friendship had failed because F did not defend his absent friend when all were attacking him in a meeting 'which later cost him his job'. Although Jean-Marc felt relieved after the parting, with the friendship he lost something important: the remembrance of himself in former years which he cannot preserve alone. Here we have the motif of 'disgust' which for Marc seems to be bound up with the notion of the beautiful body as a 'secretion machine' (10): 'For me all it takes is seeing how her eye blinks, seeing that movement of the eyelid over the cornea, and I feel a disgust I can barely control' (11). Jean Marc does not recall this 'absurd idea', contrary to the friend whom he is visiting on his death bed. But he knows that 'this is the real and the only reason for friendship: to provide a mirror so the other person can contemplate his image from the past, which, without the eternal blah-blah of memories between friends, would long ago have disappeared' (11). The friend reminded him of what he said at the age of seventeen.

> Friendship is indispensable to man for the proper function of his memory. Remembering our past, carrying it with us always, may be the necessary requirement for maintaining, as they say, the wholeness of the self. To ensure that the self doesn't shrink, to see that it holds on to its volume, memories have to be watered like potted flowers, and the watering calls for regular contact with the witnesses of the past, that is to say, with friends. They are our mirror; our memory; we ask nothing of them but that they polish the mirror from time to time so we can look at our selves in it (43).

Jean-Marc speculates in connection with this whether he would still regard friendship as the supreme value, as he did in his youth. Today he would be ready to 'choose the truth over friendship' (44). But that is less on the level of truth than on the loss of perspective for friendship in modernity. From Achilles to Dumas' musketeers there are models where friendship was stronger 'than ideology, than religion, than the nation'. Friendship arose out of an 'alliance against adversity' and was sustained as an alliance over and above oppositions, but in the world of anonymous threat from circumstances, offices and laws, this alliance has no function:

What can a friend do for you when they decide to build an airport outside your windows, or when they fire you? If anyone helps you, again it's somebody anonymous, invisible, a social-service outfit, a consumer watchdog organization, a law firm. Friendship can no longer be proven by some exploit . . . We go through our lives without great perils, but also without friendship . . . Because friendship emptied of its traditional content is transformed these days into a contract of mutual consideration, in short, a contract of politeness (45f.).

Chantal can gain something from this reflection; a friend shows himself in tact rather than in the heroic gesture. But that reintroduces the male model of friendship into a network of relationships that is customary with women.

The philosophy of friendship points up identity as a question of solidarity and memory. We seek in the friend solidarity in memory. And this is in turn selective. The novel pursues this theme of selective ideas a great deal, especially as its main figures react to unselected reality with abhorrence and loathing. Thus these are 'Platonic' people. They set the idea above reality. That has an effect on the philosophy of love. Love selects and transforms. It makes incomparable that which after all can be compared. But if the gaze no longer selects, it levels down. The beloved becomes those men who no longer turn round, the beloved becomes the woman as the plaything of suppressed needs. That is a plea for a Platonic, idealizing way of looking. It does not mean a farewell to the body or a flat dualism but the longing for an identity which cannot be calculated and summed up, which does not insist on my claim to myself but which hangs easily and naturally as a fruit on the tree of love, albeit a fruit with all the ambivalence of paradise. The gaze of love, it is said, 'rips out of society' (36). Here society consists in the juxtaposition of the contradictory: family conventions and the disillusionment of all profiles in the attraction and the artifices which are needed to sustain him.

Kundera has written a narrative which is about both identity and love at the same time. Here not all the facets of moral identity may become clear. But this central reflection of identity does appear as a moral provocation: identity not only to take but also to give, or to allow oneself to be given.

IV. The implicit readers or the mirror of society

Modern literature asserts its autonomy from society. This also includes a distancing from utilitarian applications which could be derived from literary products. On the other hand, literature has within itself society as its potential readership. Whether one asks what literature betrays about this society (as Roland Barthes does) or whether one asks about the implicit readers (as Wolfgang Iser does), one can agree that literature reckons on reflection, and one can make this speculation visible.

In Kundera's novel the figures for identification are a childless unmarried couple approaching the mid-life crisis, somewhere between thirty-five and forty-five, detached from conventional family life ('clan') and from unstable single-sex relationships. The couple signalizes a snapshot of a society in upheaval, which is expressed especially in the vicinity of media culture, of which the representative here is the advertising agency. The couple live between two conventions, the traditional and the world of diversion through manufactured euphoria, where, to quote Tomas Bernhard, one celebrates life as diversion from one's own existence. In the first instance identity is fixed with intolerable clarity; in the second case it is not there, since one is as random as the context requires – sometimes this way, sometimes that. Chantal decides her attitudes in this way, now opting for competence, at another time for self-presentation. Not even sexual attraction in advertising is stable, as the professional Leroy explains. It has to be alienated. One example is the erotic suggestions made by baby care.

Thus the implicit readers are 'carried off' into a situation which they interpret as uncertainty between offers of identification that are either too stable or too unstable. With the formal artifices of the story this uncertainty is reinforced, but saving motifs (the saving voice of the beloved) are also offered. Only these cannot provide the guarantee for the success of the identity, because the consistent and continuous 'gaze' of love is impossible for human beings and, though broken, cynical, perhaps as mere convention, allows the question of God.

Identity, it seems, can no longer be communicated in the implicit society; it can only be achieved fragmentarily by life-style. Internal biography, one's own life story, releases the memory and the utopia for one's own identity, but at the same time also everything that constantly endangers this identity by another possible identity. Chantal can slip into a social identity; Jean-Marc can hardly slip into a homeless itinerant existence. The support which love gives them is their inner norm, to constitute and preserve the identity of the other. Only imagination can achieve this, for only on this level is there the gaze of the idea without perception of the movement of the eyelid, as it were experience without empiricism, experience without exact perception.

Thus the implicit recipient is confronted with a model which does not simply depict a possible imitation but first of all provokes enlightenment.

The offer of the narrative is unemphatic, but the reader cannot evade it either; this can give rise to an individual controversy, spark off an identification (not necessarily with this model). Here the catalyst is in the 'normal' process of reading, not as the presented, analytically dissected, the sequence of scenic images which are visualized in an almost cinematic way, because one always only has before one the segment of the subjective block field. The author avoids objective descriptions; the narrator emerges only to make one uncertain of his own role, since in fact, as can be demonstrated from the text, he does not know when dream has become reality or vice versa. The narrator is not sovereign and omniscient. Therefore no recipe is to be expected from him. Rather, readers are free to identify themselves and to distance themselves. This freedom makes them uncertain, and the uncertainty can become a mere attraction or a place of reflection. Ultimately the snapshots of the narrative are not a 'proper' story, but an invitation to seek one. Motifs and constitutive elements are, however, offered for this.

V. A narrative ethic

Can one call a novel like Kundera's *Identity* a narrative ethic? If we define ethics as a reflective history of morality, the question then is how far narrative is a form of reflection. Writers like Robert Musil were certainly of this opinion. And in fact we find much narrated reflection in modern authors like Kundera. That it is presented in a vivid form of language which is easy to grasp and often uses dialogue form may be regarded as a model here. The novel is an ethic in so far as it reflects on ethics in narrative. However, the question is in what way it does this.

This narrative ethic is not the foundation for any norm, nor does it inculcate any virtues. That is, unless we were to follow Ernst Bloch in describing virtues as 'pictures of attitudes', a kind of binding quality in that which is not binding, because they remain deliberative and await creative appropriation. It seems clear that here we have an ethic of the good life, the question of the success and happiness of one's own form of life. However, this ethic is not prescriptive; it is an offer. If it follows a model of counselling, this is non-directive counselling. Wherein then does the obligatory lie in the optional?

First of all, the aesthetic experience which the novel leaves behind as a scenario that is reflected on seems to be more obligatory. Readers cannot evade it, because they agree to the reading, previously selecting a writer, buying a book, etc. The work of art provokes an aesthetic experience, i.e. the stimulating, beguiling enjoyment of the implicit reader. Readers ask, with the protagonists of the narrative, about right or wrong, loyalty and betrayal, respect and instrumentalization in relation to one another. The moral motifs are not peripheral to the aesthetic motifs: moral and aesthetic experience meet, rather, in the mode of experience, i.e. in the reflective working out of perceptions, experiences and encounters. The question of the form of life once again emphasizes the neighbourliness and this interrelationship. Nevertheless the undivided remains open to distinction.

In moral experience there is a need for ordering according to the binary code of good/evil, etc. Nevertheless the process of experience remains open to results. But the aesthetic form presses for moderate partisanship. The Platonic identity which Kundera celebrates aesthetically become morally infectious. But it can also provoke resistance, since the reflection breaks the surrogate character of the narrative, in a quite stimulating way. In any case we, as readers ourselves, become witnesses of a process of self-discovery from which we can free ourselves. We are not persuaded into an identity, but we can hardly suppress the question of what our identity is and how we are responsible for it.

If we combine this narrative ethics with a kind of philosophy of literature, for this is indeed a philosophical interpretation, where here is the trace of the theological question? It lies more on the level of play with talk of God, with God as *eventualis*. Here arises the question of a credible inculturation of faith in the face of the decline of God: talk on the one hand and the limits of the possibility of making a successful life on the other.

Translated by John Bowden

Note

Milan Kundera, *Identity*, translated by Linda Asher, is published by Faber and Faber 1998. References are given by page numbers in the text.

Bibliography

H. Kramer, *Integrative Ethik*, Frankurt am Main 1992
D. Mieth, *Dichtung, Glaube und Moral*, Mainz 1976
——— , *Epik und Ethik*, Tübingen 1976
——— , *Moral und Erfahrung*, Fribourg CH 1, 1977 reissued 2000; 2, 1998
P. Ricoeur, *Time and Narrative* (3 vols), Chicago 1990
R. Zerfass (ed.), *Erzählter Glaube – erzählende Kirche*, QD 116, Freiburg 1988 (with bibliography)

Tübingen studies on narrative ethics from the last decade

Andreas Mersch, *Ästhetik, Ethik und Religion bei Hermann Broch*, Frankfurt am Main 1989

Walter Lesch, *Imagination und Moral. Interferenzen von Ästhetik, Ethik und Religionskritik in Sartres Literaturverständnis*, Epistemata LXIII, Würzburg 1989

Jean-Pierre Wils, *Ästhetische Gute. Philosophisch-theologische Studien zu Mythos und Leiblichkeit im Verhältnis von Ethik und Ästhetik*, Munich 1990

Regina Ammicht-Quinn, *Von Lissabon nach Ausschwitz. Paradigmawechsel in der Theodizeefrage*, Fribourg CH 1991

Werner Ego, *Abschied von der Moral. Eine Rekonstruktion der Ethik Robert Musils*, Fribourg CH 1992

Walter Lesch and Matthias Loretan (eds), *Das Gewicht der Gebote und die Möglichkeiten der Kunst. Kieslowskis ,,Dekalog" – Filme*, Fribourg CH 1993

Christoph Geliner, *Weisheit, Kunst und Lebenskunst. Hermann Hesse und Bertolt Brecht*, Mainz 1998

Rule Haker, *Moralische Identität. Literarische Lebensgeschichten als Medium ethischer Reflexion. Mit einer Interpretation der 'Jahrestage' von Uwe Johnson*, Tübingen 1999

Marcus Duwell, *Ästhetische Erfahrgung und Moral. Zur Bedeutung des Ästhetischen für die Handlungsspielraume des Menschen*, Fribourg CH 1999

Christian Schenk, *Ästhetik – Ethik – Theologie. Friedrich Schiller im rezeptions-ästhetischen Diskurs*, Mainz 2000

Personalized Identity in an Individualized Society

ALBERT W. MUSSCHENGA

Introduction

What must strike every observer of modern individualized societies is the degree to which people wrestle with their 'self', their 'personal identity', how they really are deep down. In this wrestling, people's relations with others and with the society in which they live hardly seem to play a role. And that worries many observers. Does not the danger threaten that a society in which people are preoccupied with seeking their 'selves' will fall apart? Another question about which observers are worried is the danger of the fragmentation of 'the self'. People fulfil all kinds of social roles, and of necessity or of their own free will move within all kinds of social networks which often pose conflicting demands; they live in a complex, dynamic, constantly changing society and often want to lead dynamic lives themselves. How then can they still form a unity, be of one piece?

In this article I want to discuss the question what is special about the personal identity of people in an individualized society, and what the opportunities and threats are.

I. Identity

If we are to be able to speak adequately about the personal identity of people in an individualized society we need a differentiated vocabulary of concepts. The term 'identity' has different meanings, which also come through whenever we talk about personal identity.

The first meaning is that of complete equality. There are two forms of complete equality. The first is qualitative equality. One may expect two examples of the same product to be alike in quality. But they are different examples. They are not numerically identical. And that is the second form of complete equality. Even identical twins are different, singular persons, though in respect of qualities (qualities, character, appearance) they have much in common with each other. A discussion has now been going on for centuries in philosophy about what it is that makes it possible for persons or things to be numerically the same despite all the changes that they undergo. Focussed on persons: is it their body, or their memories, or is it remaining the same independent entity?

The second meaning of identity is singularity, that by which someone or something is what he or she or it is, that which characterizes them. Singularity suggests above all characteristics which distinguish someone or something from persons or things, but that is too limited an approach. It is about all the characteristics which make someone or something what they are, and thus includes the characteristics that they have in common with other persons or things.

The third meaning of identity is unity. First of all in the sense of an integrated whole of parts which go together, unity as wholeness; then unity in the sense of what binds together the different phases in the existence of entities which are subject to change – especially living beings.

1. Personal and social identity

As an outsider, one can describe a human being as a totality of physical characteristics, psychological dispositions (character traits), desires, capabilities, values and ideas. That is the human being's singularity or distinctiveness. But people also have a view of themselves, a self-concept, an image, which need not fit in with what outsiders say of them. People magnify some of their characteristics, play down others, and again do not see others at all. Part of the characteristics that they do see do not fit into the picture of the persons they want to be, and others do. They identify with those characteristics which do fit. I would call all physical characteristics, character traits, dispositions, desires and ideas a person's core self. The core self points to what a person thinks he or she essentially is and what he or she also wants to be and/or become. The core self is thus an ideal self. I shall also use the term personal identity for this core self.

People manifest themselves outwardly in a diversity of natural duties (father, mother, child), obligations (work) and voluntary social roles (in politics or leisure activities). Others gain a picture of them through this. The formation of images can also be influenced by deliberately and strategically presenting oneself in a particular way. The way in which people present themselves in and through social roles also determines the image that they present to others, let us say their social identity.

The relationship between personal and social identity is dependent on the type of society. Under the influence of the process of modernization, deep changes are taking place in the way in which personal identity relates to individuality and social identity, and thus in the nature and content of personal identity.

2. Individuation

The process of social change which has taken place in Western society since the Middle Ages is often denoted by the term 'modernization'. I shall content myself with a rough sketch of its main features. The process of modernization takes place at the levels of both the social structure and the culture to which people belong. At the level of social structure we see among other things that society differentiates itself into diverse, relatively autonomous, social spheres like the economy, politics, law, religions, etc. Coupled with that is an increasing division of labour, and specialization in social and economic life. At the cultural level, we first of all see changes in individuation, the way in which people regard themselves as individuals. Then we perceive a development in normative thinking about the relationship between individual and society which leads to the formation and articulation of what I call 'values of individuality'.

What do I mean by 'changes in individuation'? In the Middle Ages people were incorporated into the social order through their place and their family. Their life was structured by the obligations that this social position involved. Such a life offers less room for what we now call individuality. Individuality can then only be expressed in the way in which one fulfils one's role and meets one's obligations. In other words, individuality is then the way in which the individual gives form to the general – the social roles. Individuality in the sense of a singularity which distinguishes one from others was not a goal that people aimed at in this time. They wanted to be a good farmer, smith, butcher, count, etc. In the period after the eighteenth century the identification of individuals with their social position and the roles associated with them became weaker. Individuality came to be seen purely as specification, instantiation of the 'human being as such'. In the next stage individuals began to see that the process of individuation rested on themselves. Individuality became self-indicating. From that moment the goal of individuation became being a special, unique and incomparable individual.

The individual was no longer primarily seen as part of a whole. Whatever makes individuals who they are, whatever role society may play in their individuation, according to Niklas Luhmann they have their standpoint within themselves and outside society. Individuals must identify themselves by referring to the characteristics that distinguish them from others. Self-perceptions and self-descriptions can no longer be based on social position and membership of a group or community. According to authors like Beck and Giddens, the personal identity which is still constituted in pre-modern societies by shared local traditions has become an individual and reflective project. Individuals are responsible for their 'selves'; they are what they make of themselves.

The changes in views of individuation are expressed in and legitimated by the 'values of individuality'. I distinguish six of theses. First of all there is the intrinsic worth or dignity of the individual. By this I mean that individuals have intrinsic worth and do not derive that worth from their membership of a group or community. The second value is self-determination. Positive self-determination means that individuals are in a position to determine themselves rationally by a critical attitude to traditions and conventions, but also to the needs and longings of their inner nature. Negative self-determination entails freedom from external limitations and hindrances. Closely related to self-determination is the third value of personal responsibility for the consequences of one's deeds and more generally for one's life as a whole. The fourth value is authenticity, which presupposes a 'self' that must be found, unfolded or developed. The fifth is uniqueness and the sixth privacy: the value of having a place, a sphere of action in which one is free from the unwanted physical, psychological and visual interference of others. I shall not be going into the inter-relationships between these values. Together they do not form a homogeneous and harmonious ethic, but rather a pool of related but sometimes conflicting and sometimes incommensurable values.

3. Changes in personal identity

The conceptual apparatus developed in the previous section puts us in a position to identify more precisely the changes that are taking place. Perhaps the changes in individuation influence the nature of the picture that individuals have of themselves – their 'self-concept' – but we may assume that they are influential above all in the nature of their personal identity understood as 'core self'. I would describe the core self as what we think we essentially are and what we want to be or become or think we need to become. In an individualized society, people's view of who they essentially are, want to be and become, or think they must become, is to a large degree influenced by the above-mentioned values of individuality. They form the normative frameworks and indicators of the 'project' of our personal identity which we each must bring to a good end for ourselves. Remarks often heard like, 'You must lead your own life', 'You must do what suits you best', 'You must be authentic', bear witness to the effect of this. And in American TV series, young people who worry about who they are and how others regard them are assured, 'You're special.' 'You're not just anybody' is the implicit message in that kind of statement.

I see two different typical movements which people (can) take in search of their core self in modern – or if, you like, late-modern or postmodern – society. In the first case the journey leads outwards, and people seek themselves by constantly breaking through their barriers and limitations, by doing everything they can do, being everything they can be and having everything they can have. In the second case, the journey takes them inwards, to the place where they think that they can find their 'deepest self'. The changes in views of personal identity also have an influence on the relationship between personal and social identity. Social identity can become the wavelength of personal identity in the sense that individuals use their public appearance in all kinds of roles as part of their quest for their core self and or to give expression to it. Or social identity is the totality of social roles that an individual must fulfil in order to be able to function in society, but which stand apart from the person that a person thinks that he or she is or wants to be, i.e. their core self. The danger inherent in the first quest is that it leads to what has often been called the fragmentation of the self, in which individuals finally lose themselves. The second quest also has a danger, namely that individuals lose themselves because the authentic and deepest self that they seek keeps escaping them.

II. The boundless self and the danger of fragmentation

Some people are constantly occupied in discovering and investigating possibilities for themselves. Here they do not feel bound by any tradition or convention. They have the idea that one can and must be able to do everything, try everything and be everything. No talent, capacity and chance may remain unexploited. They see themselves as it were as a gold mine of which all the veins – rich and less rich – must be opened up and exploited. Or as an actor who plays various roles as a result of which she can bring before the footlights and develop the different facets and corners of her personality. Or as a graphic artist who discovers himself in and through his creations. That can result in what at least to outsiders seems to be a remarkable combination of sometimes conflicting elements, roles and convictions. A nice example of this, reported some time ago in the Dutch newspapers, was an official at the Ministry of Defence who in his leisure time was a hooligan and joined in fights between groups of supporters. There are people of whom observers ask whether they have any personal identity. And we cannot rule out the possibility that some people never ask themselves the question at all. They may have a personal identity in the sense that they identify with particular characteristics, desires and capacities that they have, but when they do this, they do it only temporarily and contextually. Their personal identity, their core self, is then that with which they identify themselves at a given moment in a concrete context. They are to be compared with someone who is constantly and hopelessly in love and loses himself in different persons, depending on the time and place. The identity of this type of person is dynamic, changeable and boundless. Because their core self lacks consistency and stability in the eyes of outsiders, it is diametrically opposed to what many people understand by having a personal identity. The development of this type of personal identity is also possible only within a society in which people play different social roles in geographically different social contexts. In a traditional local community people simply would not tolerate capricious and inconsistent behaviour from one another, because then they would no longer know what to make of someone: how far that person was trustworthy.

This type of person is constantly exposed to the danger of not being able to make any connection between the different and sometimes competing temporal and contextual manifestations of personal identity. Coherence is after all not a given, but must be constructed in the story or stories that people tell about their lives. By means of these stories people must try to make the connections between all these manifestations of themselves and enable others to understand them.

III. The evasive self and the danger of egocentricity

The other movement is the movement inwards, towards the deepest real self. The presupposition that people have an essence, a real self, occurs in philosophers like Rousseau, Herder and Sartre, but above all has widely been disseminated by humanistic psychologists like Rogers and Maslow.

Those who think in terms of the real self in general overlook the presence of the other, and of society with the strait jacket of its institutions, roles and customs which are a potential threat to the possibility of being oneself. Those who lose themselves in the other and are taken up in their social roles are alienated from themselves. Those who go in search of themselves must first of all free themselves from all influences, obstacles and bonds that alienate them from their true selves, i.e. from oppressive relationships, from trade and commerce which ask all of a person, and from roles which require one to manifest oneself in a way which goes against one's deepest self. Liberation can quite literally be understood as giving up roles, breaking relationships. Some people also do that in a quite radical way. But most are content with assuming an inner distance from those roles and relations which they cannot avoid. They know that they cannot find themselves or realize themselves in these roles, and therefore look in the space, the activities, outside.

Now everyone regularly has the experience of not being able to be themselves in particular relations and situations, of having to do things which have no meaning for them, or even being forced to do things which run counter to their deepest self. But the notion that one can live authentically only when one has really found one's deepest self can drive people on endlessly. In their search they keep experiencing that 'this isn't it'; what their deepest self really is evidently remains hidden. The beckoning perspective of the real self seems to be an ever-receding horizon. Time and again the real self escapes attempts at discovery; it remains hidden.

Does the preoccupation with the quest for the true self lead to egocentricity and egotism? I said that the quest for the true self involves a critical attitude towards one's social roles and relationships. If these hinder individuals in their quest, they will either try to shake them off or – if that is impossible – adopt a detached attitude with no inner involvement. In many countries today it is easy to get out of a marriage which begins to be oppressive. But those who can find no other work will have to endure an alienating career.

Many people fear that those who seek their true self can only enter into instrumental relationships, namely relationships which help them in the quest for their true self; that they use others purely as means. In some cases that can happen. But this danger seems to me to face those who do not look for their true self but seek enjoyment, wealth and social status. The risk is more real that those who seek themselves do not see relations with others as essential, as constituting their self. Here are a couple of illustrations. First I picture a fitness room in which everyone is occupied with the same thing, but not with one another. Over against that is the image of a sports team which dedicates itself to a goal beyond the individual – playing well and winning – for which all must be involved with one another. Those in search of their deepest selves no more run the risk of being involved with others than those who are active together in a fitness room.

Does the picture change when one abandons the presupposition that the deepest self is an individual self? Holists think that we find our true selves only when we begin to see that we are part of a greater whole transcending our individuality, like nature or the cosmos. This view can lead to an experience of being bound up with others, of an unbreakable mutual dependence. That bond is not direct but goes through the whole.

In sketching out the boundless self and the evasive self I have refrained from making a substantive judgment on the ideas which underlie these two conceptions. I have made only a few remarks about the possible consequences of an orientation on these pictures of interpersonal relations. Were I to take my judgment further, it would lead me to the question whether or not the lack of the insight that people become themselves only in and through relationships with others is the fundamental defect of both views. As I said, the evasive and the boundless self are types of personal identity which one can in fact find in our society. Whether the ideas on which these types are based – for example the idea that people have a real self – are well-founded or not, there are people who look on and experience their personal identity in this way.

Translated by John Bowden

Bibliography

Ulrich Beck, Anthony Giddens and Scott Lash, *Reflexive Modernization*, Cambridge 1994, 56–109

Anthony Giddens, *Modernity and Self-Identity*, Cambridge 1991

Rom Harré, *The Singular Self. An Introduction to the Psychology of Personhood*, London 1998

Robert Jay Lifton, *The Protean Self. Human Resilience in an Age of Fragmentation*, New York 1993

Niklas Luhmann, 'Individuum, Individualität, Individualismus', in id., *Gesellschaftsstruktur und Semantik. Studien zur Wissenssoziologie*, Vol. 3, Frankfurt am Main 1989, 149–259

Albert W. Musschenga and Anton van Harskamp (eds), *The Many Faces of Individualism*, Leuven 2000

Charles Taylor, *The Ethics of Authenticity*, Cambridge, Mass. 1991

Identity: Suppressed, Alienated, Lost

FELIX WILFRED

The relegated indigenous peoples and other suppressed minority identities of ethnic, linguistic, religious and regional character have today acquired new visibility, and they clamour for global attention. The suppressed identities are of various kinds and of diverse nature.[1] By way of example, we may refer here to the indigenous identities of the Indios of Americas, the Aborigines of Australia, the Maori people of New Zealand, the people of Hokkaido in Japan, and those who are discriminated against and suppressed identities like the Kurds of Iraq and Turkey and the Afro-Americans of United States, the untouchables of India, the tribal populations in the various regions of Asia. Events centred on Kosovo and the experiences in the regions under the former Soviet Union are sufficient indication of how seriously we need to reckon with the issue of suppressed and alienated identities today. These various identities and their aspirations could not be rooted out either by totalitarian socialism or by hegemonic statism.

Globalization, no doubt, has created instantaneous communication networks and has made our world shrink. The trajectory it projects for the future of our globe would be most welcome, but for the fact that the process of globalization has left out of its purview the reality of collective identities in the various parts of the world and nations. Any project for the future has to take realistic account of the fact that our world is made up of identities. Those identities are in themselves a positive wealth of the human family, but they are progressively being turned into negative and competing identities. The traditional multi-cultural and multi-ethnic societies are undergoing a crisis, now that the conditions in which they forged positive relationships with each other over many centuries are vanishing, and they are thrown into a world which on the surface is becoming one, but in reality is undergoing serious disintegration. This state of affairs forces us to rethink crucial issues like the practice of democracy, equality and justice in multicultural and multiethnic societies. Here is something very different from the model of a society in which the autonomous individual would be the point of reference for democracy and the practice of justice, as presupposed, for example, in John Rawls' scheme of things.[2]

I. Reasons for and agents of suppression, alienation and loss of identities

No one can seriously contest the fact that colonialism with its overt and covert practices was one of the chief historical factors that has caused the alienation, suppression and even extermination of peoples in the regions of the South. The driving out of indigenous peoples from their habitat and claiming their lands under the dubious legal title of *terra nullius* and the playing off of one ethnic group against another to forge convenient local alliances – these are facts of history whose effects have spilled over time and have become live realities in our contemporary period. Tragedies of 'ethnic cleansing' as among Tutsi and Hutu in Rwanda are extreme examples resulting from colonial division of territories and classification of peoples, and the arbitrary carving out of nations from identities in South Asia, for example, owes much to colonial practices, discourses and constructions.

The colonial legacy has been continued in many regions of the South by the states which for different reasons suppress the various identities subsumed within their respective territories. The state-sponsored terrorism and violence is something these various identities today have to reckon with. There are innumerable cases of systematic and violent intervention on the part of authoritarian states to unsettle the demographic composition of one identity or another. We may think, for example, of the situation of the Tamils in the north-eastern part of Sri Lanka. The ideology of nation-state has prompted these states to steamroller the differences, sub-nationalities, and various kinds of identities within the same country, the ideal projected being one nation, one people and one culture. But, this, as we know, is an illusion, and flies in the face of all concrete experiences and evidence. Many Asian states are even averse to discourse on the different identities in their respective nations. They react violently to internationalizing the issue of the suppressed identities in their own countries. India, China, Myanmar, Bangladesh, Indonesia and a host of other countries have raised serious reservations even to the use of the expression 'indigenous peoples' in their own territories.[3] That goes hand in hand with the cultural arguments in regard to the conception and practice of human rights.[4]

Transnational capitalism with its model of development has been another important source of the alienation and suppression of the marginal groups.

Many of these peoples have lived for centuries and millennia in territories rich in natural resources. Whether it is the indigenous peoples of the Amazon forests, the tribals of India, or the indigenous groups in northern Luzon in the Philippines, there is a common pattern of displacing them from their traditional habitat in the name of development. It could be for building up dams or to extract minerals and other resources. Any resistance to these projects uprooting them from their lands and resources is termed anti-national, reason enough to persecute, suppress and even eliminate them. Quite aware of these situations, the International Labour Organization of the United Nations adopted in 1989 a convention known as 'Convention Concerning Indigenous and Tribal Peoples in Independent Countries'.[5] The document echoes the rightful claims of the indigenous peoples and suppressed minorities.

II. Inadequacies in coming to grips with the issue of identities

Even if in every case the state does not suppress the identities and minorities by the use of violence in every case, nevertheless, it subordinates them by following a policy of assimilationism. The challenge posed by the identities is cushioned by attempting to integrate them within a single national framework or common project. In the process, the weaker position in which the identities find themselves finally results in their being effectively discriminated against. In sum, the ideology of bourgeois liberal nationalism, followed by the post-colonial states, proves to be quite detrimental to the cause of the identities. It is often forgotten that eighteenth- and nineteenth-century European nationalism was the result of the affirmation of ethnic identities *vis à vis* the imperial states of the times. The situation is markedly different in the post-colonial states of the present times in which the identities are relegated to the background or trampled upon for building up the ideal of nationalism. It is then understandable why nationalist ideology in these societies, far from being of assistance to the identities, goes against their cause and interests.

Are there other conceptualizations and ideologies in which the subordinated identities would find their legitimation and recognition of their due place? Marxism believes in the progressive withering away of primordial identities as expressions of pre-capitalist societies. Socialism has aimed at welding together the working class across ethnic, linguistic and regional identities. Political liberalism is so centred on the autonomy of the individual and his (not always her) freedom that it neglects the collectivities and considerations of solidarity. One may wonder whether the issue of identities would find support in the postmodern stream of thought, since it seems to be sensitive to the question of pluralism, difference, etc. Unfortunately, that does not seem to be the case. The postmodern *discourse* on pluralism without attention to the victims and without an ethical stand geared to transformation cannot be a matter of any particular excitement for those battling with ground-realities. In fact, postmodernism seems to lack the political teeth required to deal with the complex and intriguing question of identities.[6] What postmodernism has to offer is only a vague *contemplative pluralism* and discourses on difference which all lack the necessary cutting edge. That leads us to the next consideration.

III. Claims, assertion and resistance by the subordinated identities – the dynamics

The indigenous peoples and other oppressed minorities have learnt today to rely mainly on themselves and their resources rather than expect solutions from prevailing dominant ideologies and theoretical conceptions. The praxis and strategies of those identities are multi-pronged. In several cases, their struggles are not totally new. The tribals of India, for example, have a long history of revolt and rebellion against the British colonial authorities. The oppressed identities everywhere claim their own cultural rights and aspire to a legitimate space of freedom and autonomy. The indigenous peoples and tribals claim their lands, the untouchables of India their human dignity, the religious and linguistic minorities their due share of power within the frame of multi-cultural and multi-ethnic societies.

In our world, naming is very important; it is an expression of power. Rightly, then, many oppressed groups have in recent times refused to acquiesce in the names they have been given by the *conquistadors* or other powerful segments in the society. The 'Red Indians' – a name imposed by the colonizers with a tragic history of ethnicide behind it – could not be accepted by that people who designate themselves today as the *'Indigenas'* – the indigenous, which evokes a different world and history altogether. Disparaging references such as 'Negroes' and 'Blacks' are repelled by an oppressed people who refer to themselves as Afro-Americans. The untouchables of India were condescendingly called as *harijans* (people of God) by Gandhi – an appellation they have cast aside to denote themselves as *dalits* or the broken and oppressed people. The self-designation of the various identities is itself a new source of power and a new symbol of their self-assurance.

The claims of oppressed identities are coupled with the assertion of difference. They care to distinguish themselves from others, particularly when assimilationist policies are imposed on them as a solution to their problems. In this situation, the affirmation of difference is a weapon against facile integration. Difference also becomes the entitlement, especially when this difference is the result of a history of discrimination and disadvantages. More importantly, the assertion of difference is the way through which the marginal peoples come consciously to perceive and acknowledge their collective selves. In other words, the difference is crucial for the construction of their subjecthood as the principal agent of their emancipation.

In this process of differentiation, the various symbols and rituals of tradition undergo a hermeneutical mutation. This happens through what I would call a subaltern hermeneutics, i.e., hermeneutics by the suppressed.[7] Religions present a broad avenue in this respect. We may refer here to the way the untouchables of India have tried to re-interpret the traditional Hindu tenets and symbols in order to re-invent their distinct religious identity, different from the mainline religious tradition. If we examine the various religious traditions of the world, we will discover all through history marginal groups who found their identity by a different hermeneutics of the sacred writings, the interpretation of which by the wielders of power has not helped their (the suppressed identities') cause.

Finally, there is the important question of *historiography* by the oppressed and indigenous identities. Every writing of history is a matter dealing with power (and therefore political), whether one is aware of it or not. The way history is narrated and re-constructed – which has its own biasses and judgments – affects the inter-relationship among the various groups in multi-ethnic and multi-cultural societies. Even diachronic reconstruction of history serves in practice synchronic purposes. It makes a world of difference to present-day social relationships in a multi-ethnic community whether the history of Americas starts with the pre-Columbian civilizations, the story of Australia from that of the Aborigines, or whether historiography starts with the myth of 'discovery'.

IV. Support by those in solidarity with the suppressed identities

While the suppressed and marginal peoples remain the subjects of their own struggles, they need to be supported by an ever growing number of people. The United Nations has occupied itself with this issue in an attempt to provide an international legal framework for the cause of marginalized identities and indigenous peoples.[8] Questions relating to the definition of these concepts and their application, as well as opposition from some of the states, have caused considerable hindrance in the realization of this project. Nevertheless the issue of suppressed identities and indigenous peoples have been brought to the general consciousness of the world; it goes along with the so-called 'third generation of human rights' – centred on solidarity rights.

Another form of support that could be given to the marginal identities is to pursue a policy of positive discrimination. In societies of multiple identities, this is a very important means of empowering the groups who have suffered marginalization and suppression. Thus there can be special measures by which they are offered in preference educational or employ-ment opportunities. The Indian constitution, for example, has varying degrees of legal provisions for such positive discrimination or reservation to benefit the untouchables, the tribal people and others. This policy has also met with fierce opposition on the part of the elites and privileged sections in the society. Needless to say, the disadvantages suffered all through by the marginal identities require such supportive measures, and this is the way to ensure justice and equity in societies of unequals.[9]

A third important strategy would be to build up international solidarity for the marginal and oppressed identities. As I noted earlier, most of the states are unwilling even to admit that there are sub-nationalities, minority groups and indigenous peoples in their own territories. Attempts to solve such questions within the national borders have only proved disastrous. In the spirit of the transnational character of human rights, the issue of minority identities and indigenous people calls for an international network-ing. Of course, there is a lot of room here for ambiguity and politicizing. There is the danger that such issues could be exploited by vested interests to run down a state or a nation. But that should not deter the seriously engaged and concerned people and groups from attracting international attention wherever indigenous peoples are suppressed. Through a process of alterna-tive globalization of solidarity, the cause of the suppressed identities could be served effectively.

V. Conclusion: What could possibly be the Christian contribution?

What is the stance of Christianity *vis à vis* suppressed identities? What contribution could it possibly make to the struggles of these identities to regain their dignity, rights and selfhood? Christian history is a mixture of active involvement for the cause of marginal identities as well as of conspicuous silence in the face of brutal atrocities and genocide. Examples are not far to seek in history. It may not be difficult to find even cases of active collaboration with forces involved in destroying ethnic identities.

On the other hand, we know that the whole Bible concerns itself concretely with the reality of identities. The biblical God was a companion in the identity-formation of a 'people' without identity and power. The same God was actively involved in the post-exilic period in reconstructing the symbols and the collective identity of the battered people. The vision and world-view of Jesus and his praxis is one of helping to construct the suppressed identities of the *anawim* relegated to the backyard of history by the power-centres of Palestine as well as of the Roman Empire. Paul and his associates battled for a space for the Gentiles within early Christianity and upheld their identity against the Judaizers. The apocalyptic literature depicts in symbolic expressions the assertion of identity by those driven to the margins by the imperial sway of power.

The semantic axis of the Bible, in short, leaves us with the clear message of an option for suppressed, alienated and lost identities. For it is ultimately God's own concern. There is also a deeper reason for this option. It has been consistent with the Christian revelation that the voice of God is heard at the margins. The centres of all kinds have been identified with idols whose noise fills the place, leaving no room for the subtle voice of the true God. It is at the margins, to the powerless and suppressed identities, that God's Word reveals itself. Hence for Christians and Christian communities, moving to the margins means positioning themselves to listen to the speaking of God through the struggles and experiences of suppressed identities, indigenous peoples and minority groups. The vocation of Christians is to be permanently at the margins with God and the oppressed ones.

The difference which the various identities and suppressed groups represent is something willed by God who also willed the bio-diversity in our world. Therefore, no Christian or Christian community could subscribe to a vision of reality that tends to abolish differences under the pretext of a pseudo-unity. The word 'communion' is often referred to the inner relationships in the Christian communities. But the reality and conception of community has a much wider significance if we understand the future of the human family itself as a *communion of communities*. The Christian communitarian dimension should have this as its goal. Just as the difference between woman and man is precisely the basis for their intimate union and celebration of life, the differences in the human community become the basis for the true unity of the human family and its bliss. Hence fostering difference – especially as embodied in the suppressed groups and identities – and nurturing it is a contribution to true unity and promotion of life.

The fostering of difference entails also the obligation to involve oneself for the practice of justice specially as understood from the biblical perspective as caring for and being in solidarity with the weaker ones. The challenge today is to give expression to this understanding of justice in multi-cultural and multi-ethnic societies by being one with the suppressed and marginalized identities, In sum, Christians today should not shy away from the thorny issues of ethnic, linguistic and regional identities, but should involve them-selves in the issue of difference and everywhere give unambiguous support to any political, legal or social measures in favour of battered identities.

Notes

1. In Western societies, there are the so-called neo-tribes of identities (youth-groups, sub-cultural groupings, etc.) with an alternative life-style which have proliferated since the dramatic cultural changes of the 1960s. It is true that they remain marginal identities in Western society, but their genesis and dynamics are quite different from the suppressed identities in other parts of the world. For an illuminating study of the identity question of these neo-tribes, cf. Kevin Hetherington, *Expressions of Identity, Space, Performance, Politics*, London and New Delhi 1998.
2. Cf. John Rawls, *A Theory of Justice*, Cambridge, Mass. 1971.
3. The category of 'indigenous peoples' requires conceptual and legal clarification. In the narrow sense it applies to those peoples who have become victims as the result of European conquest, immigration and settlement into their territories. But analogically and in a larger sense the expression could be applied to the inter-ethnic situations in many countries.
4. Cf. Joanne R. Bauer and Daniel A. Bell (eds), *The East Asian Challenge for Human Rights*, Cambridge 1999.
5. Cf. Ian Brownlie (ed.), *Basic Documents on Human Rights*, Oxford[3]1997, 303–16.
6. Felix Wilfred, *From the Dusty Soil. Contextual Reinterpretation of Christianity*, Madras 1995: Ch. 18, 'Postmodernism with Teeth', 327–45.
7. Cf. Felix Wilfred, 'Towards a Subaltern Hermeneutics. Beyond the Contemp-orary Polarities in the Interpretation of Religious Traditions', in *Voices from the Third World*, Ecumenical Association of Third World Theologians, Vol. 19, no 2, 1996, 128–48.
8. Cf. United Nations, Draft Declaration on the Rights of Indigenous Peoples, 20 April 1994. Cf. Henry J. Steiner and Philip Alston (eds), *International Human Rights in Context*, Oxford 1996, 1011–16.
9. Cf. Oliver Mendelsohn and Upendra Baxi (eds), *The Rights of Subordinated Peoples*, Delhi 1994.

Business Identity through Ethical Orientation

ANNETTE KLEINFELD

I. Introduction: corporate identity – more than a cosmetic image?

The term 'corporate identity' is in fashion again. In view of the far-reaching changes which face business in a globally networked world on the threshold of the twenty-first century, interest is increasing in the so-called 'soft themes', which are usually taken to include business culture and corporate identity. A comprehensive integrative understanding of the shaping of identity by businesses as social, complex systems conditions the embedding of the business culture which has grown up or controversy with it and also the social and cultural environment. This begins with questions like: 'What will we stand for and what not?' 'What offer of meaning and, resulting from that, what possibilities of identification can we offer our employees?' 'Where are our specific potentials for creating value?' 'What contribution to the common good do we make with our products and services?'

In the changed conditions of a competitive global market the shaping of business identity and the development of culture understood in this sense also presuppose a deliberate orientation on ethical values and principles. The following (back)grounds can be identified here:

Potential customers are increasingly reacting with moral sensitivity and there is a critical public which – supported by NGOs like Greenpeace – can put massive pressure on businesses where they engage in activities which are problematical either ecologically or in other ethical respects.

There is a lack of generally binding (ethical) value orientations not only at an international but also at a national level (change of values, pluralism, the dwindling influence of authorities which traditionally communicated values, like the church).

However, successful leadership and work in the businesses of the future, i.e. in networked structures with little hierarchy within a framework of temporary deterritorialized working communities, presupposes orientation on common goals and values and the development of a culture of trust on the basis of reliable reciprocal expectations of action.

Increasing importance is attached to people as a 'whole personality', to safeguard the competitiveness of businesses and their success: profiles of requirements are shifting increasingly from competence in methods and special skills to personal and social competence, which as well as ability to be part of a team more and more include co-operative intercultural and ethical competence.

A global economic and socio-political framework is anticipated by acts of voluntary commitment.

There is an ever-increasing rate of economic criminality, which necessitates preventive measures to reinforce moral integrity and observance of the law at both an individual and an institutional level.

Grappling with these new ethical challenges and the institutionalization of adequate ways of dealing with them in business (= corporate ethics) could, I would argue, make an important contribution to the development of a healthy business culture, which in turn could be the basis for shaping a substantial business identity, a corporate identity in the true sense.

II. Culture as management of values

Businesses are not specific organizations which can be directed in a technocratic way but social systems with their own cultural identity, because they are run by men and women, and men and women are essentially-value related.[1] What does that mean?

In philosophical anthropology, Max Scheler speaks of human beings as 'value related'[2] in three respects:

in so far as they are vehicles of the supreme value, personal dignity;
in so far as they have a 'natural' need for values which give their existence a support, orientation and meaning;
in so far as they have a capacity for 'perceiving' and 'feeling' values[3] and thus can relate to existing values in a critical and reflective way.

Above all this last point sheds new light on human beings as mediators between different (sub)cultures and their particular values. To the degree to which employees identify with a business, they become vehicles of its values, and what is culture-specific for them becomes the normative orientation. This makes values an instrument of leadership by which the action and behaviour of employees can be influenced.

At the same time, however, values are also the starting-point for the deliberate shaping and development of business cultures. For to be a vehicle of values does not mean becoming the sealing-wax for random forms of social or business cultures. The specific nature of human personalities consists rather in once again being able to relate in critical reflection to the cocktail of natural drives, inherited patterns of behaviour and diverse secondary and tertiary socio-cultural shaping, and to define by oneself what are to be the orientations of one's life. This particular capacity for autonomy which makes up human freedom, combined with the ability to know values, also makes it possible to decide on the values which prevail within a social situation at a particular time, in order in this way to influence its specific culture.

It is true of the culture of social systems like businesses, as it is of human personality, that it evades any objectifying approach from outside. Human personality cannot be grasped and therefore comprehended, but can always only be inferred, on the one hand by following and sympathizing in an understanding way with its intentions, i.e. its purposes, opinions, desires, hopes and anxieties, etc., and on the other by the way in which it shapes its life, by means of the values and principles by which it performs its thought and action. Business cultures too can be experienced and disclosed only by means of particular phenomena like working-methods, style of communication, climate, etc. Only by acceding to this – in holistic acts of 'feeling values', in Scheler's sense – does one have the chance to get through to the common cultural possession which governs action and behaviour.

Thus values are the starting point for the further development or focussed transformation of the culture and identity of a business.

The first step is to bring these values to consciousness, to reflect critically on them and to relate them to one another. It is precisely here that one of the two essential values of ethics lies, which at the same time represents the necessary condition for its second task: a normative determination of these values, i.e. the establishment of binding values and principles which *should* guide the actions of all men and women within a social system.

III. Identity through ethical commitment

To the degree to which members of social systems acknowledge ethical orientations and direct their action by them, the reliability of mutual expectations of action and behaviour increases. This is one of the decisive factors in forming trust and thus in turn – economically speaking – through supervision and control mechanisms lowering the costs of transactions which arise. Ethics is indispensable for the smooth and efficient functioning of societies and their sub-systems. Independently of this purely functional significance, however, for businesses there is a series of other good reasons for being concerned about an ethical orientation.

For morally relevant questions arise wherever people act and decide, and where other people or life-systems are affected by the results of their activities. In so far as businesses are themselves social systems, and interact with other social systems and people, they do not operate in a vacuum, i.e. a value–neutral moral-free area. To recognize this, i.e. to perceive oneself as part of a more comprehensive social context and as set over against other social systems, is a necessary ingredient of the act of becoming self-aware, which is as essential for the formation of a corporate identity as it is for the discovery and formation of identity in human individuals.

Businesses become 'viable' systems in the real sense only by being made up of people who as members of an organization put their specifically human capacity for action and decision at the service of the entrepreneurial aim. So economic action is human action and as such is always morally responsible. To the same degree and for the same reasons why businesses are capable of action, they are thus also morally responsible and also morally capable of responsibility; namely on the basis of the personality and morality of their members.[4]

However, the human being as a person is not only the subject of ethical action but at the same time faces moral responsibility. Businesses are therefore ethically obligated both to the external partners with which they interact and to reference groups – customers, suppliers, public, the natural environment – and also internally to their own members.

In the first place here there is the recognition and observance of ethical principles which cannot be transgressed, like the recognition and pre-servation of personal dignity, the respect for human freedom and self-determination or corresponding individual rights, etc. From these follow non-negotiable human claims and moral obligations which apply equally and *a priori*, beyond any cost-benefit considerations, to all stakeholders in a business. However, especially in international contexts, the unconditional validity of particular principles does not simultaneously coincide with their actual validity. In the course of globalization, cultural circles and the values that go with them get mixed. The ethical standards in justice, law and the prevailing morality which over the course of time have become established in Western societies cannot be immediately presupposed as generally binding in African or Asian countries. However, that does not alter the fact that there are ethical norms which make a justified claim to unconditional and thus *global* validity beyond culture-specific convictions. Ethical orientation means going by these.

No system-immanent motivation can be found for ethical commitment, which does not prove to conform with the market because the conditions of a political order are still lacking, but can initially be associated with loss of profit and competitive disadvantages, on the basis of a business rationality with a utilitarian stamp. Rather, this is a kind of voluntary self-obligation and thus – according to Kant – ethical action in the real sense. For human persons, ethical commitment of this kind is one of the decisive factors in forming their identity: for Kant, human autonomy displays itself in the realization of positive freedom by the orientation of one's own action on the 'moral law', beyond any purposive rationality.[5] If we transfer this connection to business, then by corresponding pro-active action ethical commitment makes an important contribution to strengthening corporate identity.

However, business has this capacity for 'moral' self-determination only in a secondary or analogous sense, i.e. on basis of the ethical or moral competence of its members. Only human persons owe it to themselves and their own dignity also to fulfil their professional roles in a morally responsible way. Businesses as such do not have either internal moral authorities like a conscience or guilt-feelings or special moral capacities for critical self-reference and distancing, moral power of judgment and ethical reflection.

So does the ethical orientation of businesses depend solely on the moral integrity of the responsible agents at their head?

Yes and no. The inner basic attitude of the staff of a business – at all levels – is indispensable for the successful implementation of ethical value-orientations in business: as a primitive factor to motivate those responsible for directing the business and as a presupposition for successful implementation by the firm. However, it is not sufficient in itself. Where a concern for the morally responsible leadership of a business is not an integral element of management generally, it quickly runs the risk of becoming a kind of Don Quixotery for its protagonists, which quite often results in a surrender of personal moral identity. If ethical commitment in a business is not to prove a source of friction and inner conflicts over aims, it must be rooted in business policy as a commitment specific to the firm, and also be institutionalized by appropriate measures so that it can be implemented as corporate ethics.

Only under these conditions can ethical orientation also develop its substantive significance for the formation of a credible corporate identity.

IV. Corporate ethics and corporate identity

At first sight, ethics and identity seem to be contradictory; identity draws on the specific and other, setting it apart from a particular environment. By contrast, ethics occupies itself with the orientation of individual action on the universally valid and binding. Where is the connection between them?

Context is constitutive of the definition of the identity of the human individual. This personal identity is comprised by the fact *that* it relates to others, and above all the way in which it does so. Another important factor is perceiving that one is part of a greater whole and becoming aware of how one is shaped by this surrounding world with its different cultures and value systems. That is the presupposition for giving oneself one's own direction, i.e. not allowing oneself to be shaped but to establish and define oneself. In the first place this includes a kind of standpoint in relation to the values which have guided one so far; in the second place the question of what one wants to maintain and what one does not. However, the embodiment of human self-determination is not some random choice, but orientation on what is morally justified. Both reflection on values as a form of self-knowledge and the grounding of values as the basis for self-determination are the subject of ethics.

Therefore there is no identity of social systems within other social systems without ethics. For ethics implies taking up a position, adopting a standpoint on what surrounds us and shapes us, above all on the classical ethical questions. What should we go by? By what values should our action be guided?

Related to business identity, in an analogous way ethics can provide both a contribution to the discovery of identity and to the formation of identity:

as a means of self-knowledge;
as a way towards clarity in the diversity of pluralistic world-views by basing one's own action on ethically justified 'good reasons' and principles.

The specific culture of a business is constitutive of its identity. As has been shown above, in turn this culture is crucially dependent on norms of behaviour and values which are usually present only implicitly, according to which people act in it. The establishment of a code of ethics or similar measures must necessarily precede making these values peculiar to the firm conscious and reflecting on them. To implement an ethic persistently and effectively in business, that ethic must be integrated: into the culture, into the philosophy of the firm so far, the specific orientation of the business. So the ethic must become part of its identity and be embraced by it.

This process of becoming aware of oneself is extended by the integration of ethical reflections about the question of the right and the good. This gives corporate identity and quality; by combining what is specific to a business with what is generally justified in ethical terms it becomes a 'positive' identity, i.e. one which has been reflected on morally and is self-defined. This finds adequate expression in a perception of entrepreneurial freedom which is also morally responsible, and its consistent implementation in everyday practice.

By ethical orientation a business takes on a corporate identity which is no longer random. With its acknowledgement of unconditionally valid principles, in addition it can distinguish itself in global competitive conditions from the plurality of cultural world-views. At the same time this counters the danger of an ethical relativism to which employees in transnational businesses are especially exposed. The tendency simply to adapt to the customs of the land in question is problematical in two respects: first, when employees are forced to give up their own values, and thus their personal or moral integrity is affected; and secondly, if these 'customs' are ethically questionable, like paying or receiving bribes.

A business which sets up ethical guidelines for dealing with morally relevant questions of this kind and makes them binding throughout the firm or the concern also offers its employees support in international contexts and reinforces their moral integrity. In this way it ultimately strengthens its own integrity and thus in turn its resistance to criminality and corruption and its national and international public reputation. Everyone likes to identify with a business whose identity draws on an obligation to the 'good' and to corresponding values; people like to work in it and are motivated; customers like doing business with it because it can be trusted; and consumers like to buy its products because they know that 'all is well behind the scenes'.[6]

Thus an ethically based corporate identity is at the same time the 'royal road' to a persistently positive image both internally and externally – provided that it does not stop at a declaration of intent in matters of ethics. For identity implies consistency. Where the connection between ethical self-determination and consistency is overlooked, the consequences for credibility and thus for the image of the business can, quite to the contrary, be persistently negative.

V. Ethics as risk: the Pechmarie principle

In view of the advantage which corporate ethics can bring to businesses as described above, the question of the motivation of efforts towards a business ethic seem to be clear. What then of the act of moral commitment out of inner conviction which has to precede these efforts? Is that made only because otherwise from the perspective of 'moral purists' with a Kantian stamp this would not be ethics at all? Over and above that there is also a pragmatic reason: the one – benefit – cannot be had without the other – serious conviction. Under the specific perspectives of economic and business ethics, it is quite justified for ethical business practices to pay off for a business. An interest in profit, an improvement of image, an increase in productivity, an avoidance of a lack of efficiency and costs which arise through corruption or a bad business climate – all this may very well play a role in a concern for morally responsible business practice. But as a rule the effort is doomed to failure unless at the same time there is an honest interest in what is morally right, and those responsible are motivated by a corresponding inner attitude. For there are goals which cannot be aimed at or reached directly, like happiness and a successful life. According to Aristotle, these come only to those who lead a virtuous life in the service of the city. In antiquity, virtue was regarded as the condition of a good public reputation, for a positive image. For Aristotle and for Plato this virtue consisted in referring daily actions and decisions to the superior 'idea of the good', for the sake of the good and the noble.[7]

That this attitude can ultimately also bring economic benefit is shown in the Grimm brothers' fairy tale 'Frau Holle': here the basic moral attitude of Goldmarie, who does not look for reward but acts out of a readiness to help, generosity and for the sake of the matter itself, pays off. Those on the other hand who attempt to instrumentalize ethics will fare like Pechmarie: because she only apparently overcomes her own laziness and malice with the intent of ultimately being rewarded with a gold ring like her sister, she can only be rubbed in the dirt.

In business contexts, too, there are goals which evade all purposive rationality, the attainment of which presupposes the 'detour' via an orientation on ethical values for their own sake. The development of a 'sound' business culture is an example of this, but the increased performance of employees is also a goal of this kind: the 'new human potential' which is urgently needed today to ensure the competitiveness of a business and which is often quoted can be discovered only indirectly by perceiving people not primarily in terms of their contributions or as 'resources' to be gained but as what they really are: persons, i.e. not 'something' but 'someone'.[8]

Above all in the development of a credibly corporate identity with integrity business are confronted with the ethical paradox described above. And this paradox not only implies the possibility that advantages will not materialize; at the same time corporate ethics also contains a risk, what one might call the 'Pechmarie principle'. For where a business states its ethical orientation, whether through relevant PR measures or by producing an ethical code for the firm, it can and will immediately be measured by those standards, internally by its own staff and externally by customers, suppliers and the public. One of the most important factors in creating trust in the relationship of a business to its various stakeholders is credibility, and the decisive presupposition for that is integrity. As in the case of personal integrity, the integrity of a business is first of all shown by its authenticity: by life according to its own principles. Where a business 'outs' its principles by guidelines or in brochures this integrity can much more easily be checked. Is there a consistency between what has been presented in a firm's glossy brochure and what makes up its actual culture and practice?

Where a business explicitly acknowledges ethical value-orientations, this congruence of should and is, of moral claim and reality, can be observed particularly critically. Why? Because self-consistency and integrity are themselves ethical categories which are expressed in values like honesty, incorruptibility, observance of the law, honouring agreements with third parties, keeping promises and above all in observing its self-imposed principles.

Thus any divergence between guidelines and the everyday life of the firm are clearly judged more strictly here – at least from outside and by its own workers – than in the case of a business which makes no ethical claim. However, corresponding should-is balances in the management itself are often lacking. That is usually the case when the motivation is one-sided in the sense mentioned above.

That makes the consequences all the more fatal if discrepancies become evident to others; first, because in the face of the professed ethical commitment this is a performative self-contradiction which counts double; and secondly because irresistibly – whether with justification or not – the suspicion of a misuse of ethics arises: the up-front cultivation of image is an excuse for disguising some problems. The credibility, the trustworthiness and thus the reputation of a business in the outside world are not only forfeited but permanently damaged, as is the motivation provided by a programme with an ethical foundation because it offers identity and meaning.[9]

Thus if the initiative in the direction of a strengthening of corporate identity, a good public reputation and a culture of trust which can serve corporate ethics is not to prove counter-productive, the commitment formulated in the guidelines must not be determined by these motives themselves, at least primarily and not exclusively. Ethical commitment in the real sense is shown by 1. the fact that these are taken seriously; 2. the fact that it is accompanied by an effective and consistent implementation which confirms this honesty.[10]

Only if ethical principles and values are integrated into the general philosophy and culture of a firm – and only then do we have corporate ethics in the real sense – does a business become the 'system of meaning' which offers its members the required orientation and possibility of identification even in difficult circumstances, in times of structural change and in multinational contexts. Human beings can experience meaning only when they can go by something that corresponds to their real being, their dignity as persons, namely spiritual and ethical values. According to Scheler, only values with this category also create community and cohesion, solidarity and loyalty.

Translated by John Bowden

Notes

1. For more details see A. Kleinfeld, *Persona Oeconomica. Personalität als Ansatz der Unternehmensethik*, Heidelberg 1998, 217–24.
2. Cf. N. Hartmann, *Ethik*, Berlin ²1935, 206.
3. Ibid., 205f.; cf. also M. Scheler, *Der Formalismus in der Ethik und die materiale Wertethik*, Bern 1954, 385f.
4. Cf. Kleinfeld, *Persona Oeconomica* (n.1), 117–52.
5. Cf. Kant, *Grundlegung zur Metaphysik der Sitten*, BA 85/86, Gesammelte Schriften IV, Berlin 1911, 429.
6. K. M. Leisinger, *Unternehmensethik, Globale Verantwortung und moderne Management*, Munich 1997, 183ff., also points to the growing significance attached to the 'ethical appearance' of a business as a commercially useful advantage in competition.
7. Cf. Aristotle, *Nicomachean Ethics* 1096b32, 1099a16, 1101b27, 1105a26, 1116b30.
8. Cf. R. Spaemann, *Personen. Versuche über den Unterschied zwischen 'etwas' und 'jemand'*, Stuttgart 1996.
9. For the persistent consequences of an 'ethic of life' cf. also J. Staute, *Das Ende der Unternehmenskultur. Firmenalltag im Turbokapitalismus*, Frankfurt am Main 1997, 192–7.
10. For an account of practical measures at implementation cf. A. Kleinfeld, 'Identität durch moralische Integrität: Die Rolle der Corporate Ethics', in R. Bickmann, *Chance, Identität, etc*, 371–409, esp. 402–7.

II. Philosophical Discussion

The Hermeneutical Anthropology of Charles Taylor

THOMAS GIL

Human beings have the competence to give meaning to all that they do and make by interpreting what they have done and made in the light of various projects and plans which they themselves have developed and pursued. The Canadian philosopher Charles Taylor refers to this competence when he defines human beings consistently as 'self-interpreting animals'. If human beings are 'self-interpreting' animals, then that has consequences for all those sciences which have human beings as their subject. In that case, the human sciences (the classical intellectual, social and cultural sciences) can no longer favour solely an externalized view of people, but must be concerned to develop an internalistic, hermeneutic perspective if they want to do justice to their epistemological subjects, namely human beings. For only an internalistic, hermeneutical view can do justice to the relationships of 'self-interpreting animals' to themselves and the world.

The first section will clarify precisely what this means. Then, in the second section, we shall investigate Charles Taylor's critique of 'atomistic' universalism, an understanding of human beings which developed late in history and has many presuppositions. Charles Taylor reconstructs the genesis of this human self-portrait with the intention of showing its plausibility but also its limitations. In the third and last section I shall discuss Taylor's reflections on a contemporary 'politics of recognition' based on his hermeneutical anthropology.

I. Charles Taylor's hermeneutical model of a science of the human being

Charles Taylor has published in two composite volumes on the topics *Human Agency and Language* and *Philosophy and the Human Sciences* a series of philosophical papers in which he takes up and deepens the critique of reductionist approaches in the human sciences that he had already formulated in his investigation *Explanation of Behaviour*, which appeared in 1964. At the end of *Explanation of Behaviour* Taylor argued for teleological explanations of human behaviour which take account of the fact that human beings are intentional beings who are in a position of having or pursuing aims and purposes that make sense of particular actions and cannot be embraced conceptually by the mechanistic explanatory models of actions (which are very popular in particular human sciences).

Now in his *Philosophical Papers* Taylor describes the human being as a being who makes qualitative evaluations in interpretation by which the world takes on meanings that were not there before; these evaluations can make meaningful to individuals the natural processes of life which otherwise would be neutral or indifferent to meaning. Taylor is particularly interested in the consequences of such 'qualitative discriminations' and in particular in the interpretative nature of human beings for the sciences which have human beings as their objects. Because the self-interpretations and the qualitative evaluations based on them are an important part of human life, indeed are the specifically human element in human life, the human sciences cannot be exclusively naturalistic. This is the quintessence of Taylor's argument. In other words, they cannot orientate themselves exclusively on the objectivistic models of the natural sciences and act as if there were no inner aspect or no qualitative modes of experience and dimensions of meaning in human life. In order to be able to do full justice to this inner aspect of human life, according to Taylor the human sciences must become 'hermeneutical sciences' which follow through human beings' interpretation of themselves and the world in an understanding way.

Now what does it mean specifically that human beings are living beings who interpret themselves and their world and in this way make qualitative assessments through which what is natural or indifferent to meaning can become meaningful and can bear meaning? Specifically, it means that in principle human beings are in a position to want to evaluate their own desires and aims by reflecting on them, to examine them critically and determine whether or not they want to have such desires and aims. For this activity of reflection, evaluation and criticism of human subjects, human beings have at their disposal notions, images, models and schemes which they develop and appropriate in communities; these are not already part of the equipment of the natural world, but only enter the natural world through human beings. Charles Taylor refers to Harry Frankfurt's definition of human beings as beings who can have 'second-order desires' and expands this anthropological definition by showing that such 'second-order desires', or desires about desires, are possible only on the basis of ideas and notions of one's own life and the specific way in which one wants to live it.

Thus for example certain people may have a sudden desire to smoke a cigarette. But at the same time on the basis of a health plan which they themselves have worked out and affirmed, these people can also desire not to have the first desire or first-order desire, i.e. the desire to smoke. Thus they can develop other desires in relation to their own desires which are desires about desires, second-order desires. These second-order desires are reflected desires and always presuppose images, notions, models and ideas which are important and significant to individuals and one must take that into account if one wants to understand a particular person and the way in which he or she behaves.

In other words, human subjects interpret their own life by means of images, notions, models, ideas and personal schemes which enable them to make certain assessments, and in this way subjective qualitative meanings arise. Specific developments in human life are always characterized by 'qualitative significance', a characteristic which does not follow mechanically from the endowment of the natural world but is claimed and created by human subjects in their willing.

Now the images, ideas, notions and models of themselves which human beings develop are important not only for the wishes, aims and projects of individuals; by virtue of the fact that they produce meanings in the life of those individuals they also shape the individual feelings and emotions of individuals to such a degree that one can say that human feelings or emotions are never raw feelings and emotions, but are always feelings and emotions which have already been interpreted. Thus for example the feeling of shame that occurs in people is never an abstract, absolute and universal feeling, but always already a feeling which has been modelled cognitively. Accordingly, one is ashamed of one's own ideas, self-images and models in particular situations, and on the basis of particular events which are interpreted in one way or another and accordingly have this or that relevance.

According to Charles Taylor, any objectivist ontology which does not take these qualitative characteristics into account is doomed to failure, since it can only treat reality in a reductionist way and systematically ignores important dimensions of this reality or distorts them in naturalistic programmes of explanation. On the basis of the qualitative differences which can mark the lives of individuals, a meaning of life arises along with the identity of the individuals concerned; here the individuals can only learn to develop qualitative differences, perceive them and also treasure them in communities. Charles Taylor uses two basic terms to describe this qualitative 'more' that makes up human life: 'significance' and 'import'. Both terms are subject-related or subject-relative and both denote qualities of experience in human life. At the end of his article 'Self-Interpreting Animals', Taylor sums up in five theses what is characteristic of human beings. 1. Typically human emotions always contain import-ascriptions; 2. These import-ascriptions are always relative to the subject; 3. Feelings relative to the subject are the basis of our understanding of what it means to be human; 4. Such subject-related feelings are constituted by interpretations; 5. Interpretations of human beings and the world need language.

The fifth thesis formulates an implication of all that has been said so far, namely that complex qualitative assessments and modes of experience can be had only on the basis of language. This confirms Aristotle's anthropological definition that the human being is a being that has language (*logon echon*). However, and this is important for Charles Taylor, the human being is a being which not only uses language for denotative purposes but is also in a position to practise an expressive use of language. Alongside the significance of the 'designative theory of language' which has played a normative role for the constitution of objectivizing descriptions and explanations of nature, especially in modern times, Taylor emphasizes the relevance of the 'expressive theory of language' which was developed in the course of the 'romantic revolution' and is particularly suited for communicating subjective qualitative differences and differentiations. According to Taylor, a consistent application of the designative model of language to expressions of human speech (words, sentences and texts) would amount to a programme of naturalization. This he associates with the names of B. F. Skinner, W. V. O. Quine and D. Davidson; it presupposes the complete transparency of human experiences, namely that in principle they can be understood or explained absolutely, whereas in his eyes the expressive theory of language can only follow the complex mediation of human life and its psychological dynamic in an understanding way.

The argument so far means that the human sciences cannot exclusively restrict themselves to constructing naturalistic or objectivistic models in order to depict and explain the human; they must also concern themselves with internalistic models in which the qualitative characteristics of human life come to bear. The internal view of human subjects of action and the self-interpretation of these subjects are all-important if we want to understand how human beings live out their lives in practice and how they act. Therefore the human sciences have to become hermeneutical sciences: understanding sciences in which the subjective meanings and significances of individuals have to stand at the centre of conceptual and theoretical efforts. For the human modes of behaviour which are to be explained and understood in the human sciences are modes of action which cannot be reduced to the observable, physical dimension; they always presuppose interpretations, significances, intentions, plans, shared notions and common meanings. Taylor gives three examples to illustrate what he means here: military actions, political elections and social interaction in negotiations. In the first instance one understands the movements of troops and machines only if one does not concentrate on the level of individual bodily organs, screws, motors and mechanistic apparatuses, but places the military strategies, intentions and plans at the centre and attempts to follow them through and understand them. In the second case one can understand the behaviour of the individual in action only if one knows what the social action of a political election is or means. Now this social action can be understood only in the context of a culturally-conditioned political system which has been organized according to particular ideas and notions, i.e. according to particular meanings. In the third case one can know what negotiation means only if one knows and understands the cultural practices which are summed up under this concept.

The human sciences which have to explain the three phenomena just mentioned cannot be content with working out 'thin' physicalistic theories in which human intentions and plans have no place. They must work out 'richer' theories in which 'thick' descriptions of the phenomena are possible that can do justice to the collective and subjective self-interpretations of the subjects concerned.

II. A critique of 'atomistic' individualism

In his practical philosophy Aristotle describes the human being as a being capable of speech who is also political; these two definitions belong together and point to each other. With his definition of the human being as a 'self-interpreting' animal Taylor takes Aristotle's first definition into account. Aristotle's second definition comes completely into play in Taylor's critique of 'atomistic' liberalism. For the starting point of Taylor's critique of 'atomism' is the insight that human beings cannot become human without social communities into which they are born and in which they learn language, action and thought in practice. Taylor understands by 'atomism' all those concepts in social philosophy which begin from the individual and think of the individual as a sovereign, self-sufficient subject of action endowed with instrumental rationality. For Taylor, what is particularly problematical about these 'atomistic' approaches is that in them an idea about human subjects of action which developed late in history and has many presuppositions is universalized and stylized as human nature. In other words, it is as if human beings, all human beings and in all eras, were what the 'atomistic' models describe in a naturalizing way.

In his article 'Atomism', Charles Taylor presents in an evocative form his critique of the conception of a decontextualized or 'disengaged identity' which coincides with the atomism of social philosophy. In his *magnum opus* on philosophical subjectivity, *Sources of the Self. The Making of the Modern Identity*, from 1989, Taylor then reconstructs the complex genesis of modern identity and modern conceptions of the self with the aim of demonstrating the particular validity and limitation of individual conceptions. In the article on 'Atomism', Taylor's main point of criticism is that the 'atomistic' models forget their own historical conditions and presuppositions and develop a one-sided picture of the human self in which the fundamental role of communities (of thought, language and action) for the constitution of the self is completely neglected. 'Atomistic' models, like those which have been developed by the contractualists or theoreticians of contract and some utilitarians, conceive human beings as self-interested, isolated individuals who constantly calculate how they can achieve optimal satisfaction of all their desires and preferences. The social character of these wishes and preferences, i.e. the way in which they are conditioned by history and by social culture, is systematically bracketed off in the atomistic models.

Only historical reconstructions can help to counter the forgetfulness of history or the historical short-sightedness in such models. In these reconstructions the historical, relative character of social and cultural notions is demonstrated and opposed to the illegitimate naturalizing generalizations. It is precisely this work of genetic reconstruction that Charles Taylor takes on in his *Sources of the Self*. In this work he shows dimensions of the modern identity, but also problematical aspects of some notions, like that of the 'disengaged self', which has been attacked by authors such as Merleau-Ponty, Heidegger, Wittgenstein and Polanyi – to mention just some of the names given by Taylor.

Charles Taylor's interest in a critique of one-sided naturalistic conceptions of the self is the impetus behind his work on the genealogical relativization of modern naturalism; it not only leads to negative-critical deconstruction but also points out some positive developments, like the romantic revolution or turning point which has made the image of the self more complex and deeper.

For Taylor the philosopher, Georg Wilhelm Friedrich Hegel remains a permanent point of reference. Taylor sees Hegel's philosophy of the Spirit as a complex theory of action which is in a position to form the counterpoint to modern individualistic causal theories in which the 'qualitative common meanings' that are so important for him are not given their due. In Taylor's interpretation, in Hegel's philosophy of the Spirit we have a complex qualitative theory of action which can understand the subjective and the objective dimensions of human action. Complexes of action are covered which even have their own history of origin and development.

III. Politics of recognition

In various articles Charles Taylor derives a series of practical political consequences from his own hermeneutical conception of anthropology and the humane sciences and from his critique of atomism in social philosophy; they could be summed up under the heading 'Politics of Recognition'. If it is the case that human beings always culturalize natural processes of life by interpreting them and thus making them significant, i.e. providing them with subjective meaning, then the sciences about human beings and their actions, the human sciences, have to be hermeneutical disciplines which do justice to both dimensions of human life, the objective dimension of mechanisms and functions and the subjective or intersubjective dimension of meanings and singificances. In this subjective-collective dimension of meanings, human beings develop complex, deep, culturally mediated models of meaningful humanity which are responsible for various identities and coexist side by side, compete with one another or can learn something from one another. As there is no plausible reason why particular models of a qualitative human life suppress other equally good models or make them disappear, the question arises how the various models or outlines of a good life coexist and, in the best case, can be fruitful to each other. This question is not only one of practical politics but an eminently 'political' question, since it relates to the concrete recognition or belonging or participation in a social whole: a participation with which for example the French philosopher Jacques Rancière in his book *La Mésentente. Poilitique et Philosophie*, can sum up the political.

The question of recognition or involvement (and not being excluded) is political because it implies a series of institutional and organizational consequences without which human beings cannot really develop their qualitative individual lives. Freedom always presupposes cultural milieux in which it can come into being and be experienced in practice. Similarly, human models of meaning presuppose cultural spheres with the corresponding institutional and practical conditions in which they arise, develop and are handed on. The different models each have their plausibility, i.e. their meaning and their power of conviction, in these cultural spheres. Moreover in them they can have a practical effect and develop. Therefore these culture spheres in which alone manifold and rich schemes of meaning and living can develop are to be made possible politically and encouraged.

With a glance at Jean Jacques Rousseau, Georg Wilhelm Friedrich Hegel, Johann Gottfried Herder and others, in his article 'Politics of Recognition' Charles Taylor describes how in the history of the West it has come about that there has been a transition from 'honour' as a hierachizing social principle to 'dignity' as an egalitarian social principle, and that moreover authenticity had been discovered as a moral quality. Finally the value of the individual, the subjective and the unique has become established in the various assessments of the quality of human life. On the basis of these three developments a view of human life has come into being in which it appears as a deep, complex, manifold and meaningful phenomenon which needs various external conditions and institutions for it to be able to develop as such. There is no single qualitative way of shaping human life and living it out, but many possible ways which presuppose traditions and call for particular external, social and cultural conditions. Sensitivity to the difference of the individual schemes and identities, the treasuring of the diversity of the qualitative and respect for the other are aspects of an attitude of recognition of the unique and contingent which is relative to subject and community, along with a quality of life, meaningful and significant, which makes up the complexity and goodness of human life as it is lived.

But this recognition must not just remain an intellectual attitude. It must also materialize in the social, i.e. in institutions and organizations. In this way it becomes political. As real freedom and real equality are never merely formal entities, but live by concrete material and substantial options which are to be had only in traditions and cultural patterns of actions and shapings, a liberal model of society based on freedom and equality cannot be blind to the material nature and the content of these processes.

In an article on 'Liberalism', Ronald Dworkin attempts to define what is characteristic of a liberal position. Dworkin designates by 'liberal' a theory of equality which adopts a neutral standpoint to the various concrete conceptions of the good, valuable and meaningful life, since such a neutral standpoint is the only legitimate one. Despite some differences in the conceptual definition of liberalism between Dworkin and Taylor – differences to which Charles Taylor has himself referred at different points – Charles Taylor remains a liberal philosopher and social theorist who knows the importance of content and material options for the coming into being of the good life. His plea for multiculturality is the logical consequence of his own hermeneutical, cultural and social-anthropological approach. According to Taylor, multiculturality does not mean randomness, but the concrete recognition of what is truly good, and is to be had only through cultural mediations and in the plural. Cautiously he says in connection with some reflections of Johann Gottfried Herder at the end of his article 'The Politics of Recognition':

Herder, for example, cherished the notion of a divine providence according to which the diversity of cultures did not appear as mere chance but was destined to produce greater harmony. I cannot deny that this is right. But in an elementary sense, too, it is the case that cultures which have opened up a horizon of meaning to a large number of people of different character and temperament over long periods of time – which, in other words, have given expression to their sense of what is good, holy, admirable – display something that deserves our admiration and respect, though alongside that we may find much that we must abhor and reject. Perhaps one could put it like this: it would be a sign of the utmost arrogance to exclude this possibility *a priori*.

Translated by John Bowden

Bibliography

R. Dworkin, *A Matter of Principle*, Oxford 1985

H. O. Frankfurt, *The Importance of What We Care About. Philosophical Essays*, Cambridge 1988

W. Kymlicka, *Multicultural Citizenship. A Liberal Theory of Minority Rights*, Oxford 1995

J. Rancière, *La Mésentente. Politique et Philosophie*, Paris 1995

C. Taylor, *The Explanation of Behaviour*, London 1964

——, *Hegel*, Cambridge 1975

——, *Human Agency and Language. Philosophical Papers* 1, Cambridge 1985

——, *Philosophy and the Human Sciences. Philosophical Papers* 2, Cambridge 1985

——, *Sources of the Self. The Making of the Modern Identity*, Cambridge 1989

——, *Philosophical Arguments*, Cambridge, Mass. 1997

——, *Multikulturalismus und die Politik der Anerkennung*, Frankfurt am Main 1997

Narrative and Moral Identity in Paul Ricoeur

HILLE HAKER

I. The identity of a person

1. Elements of personal identity

Personal identity can be seen from many perspectives, but the main approaches have been summarized by Paul Ricoeur as idem-identity and ipse-identity. With the first term ('identity of the same') Ricoeur refers to the tradition of identity as the identification of something or somebody *over* time. The second term, ipse-identity ('identity of the self'), refers to concepts of the self as a person *in* time.

The identity of a person requires both dimensions, which are of course bound up with each other: without identification and extension over time, we are just as unable to speak of the identity of a person as we are without the self-image, the idea of identity, that which defines us in our existence, which, however, can be captured conceptually only in terms of our life histories.

However, there is much more to be said about other elements of personal identity:

Physical immediacy

The notion of identity implies the physically immediate certainty of self which makes it impossible to treat oneself as an external object of consideration. We are our bodies, even though we have bodies about whose nature we can communicate with others. Even so, the pain, for example, that we feel concerns us directly: it cannot be considered as a phenomenon external to ourselves, and cannot be divided up or shared. It is often the case that we first become conscious of our uniqueness in our physical perceptions and impressions of ourselves; these, however, not infrequently throw us into a feeling of loneliness and abandonment which particularly Jean Paul Sartre demonstrated again and again, certainly most impressively in *La Nausée*.

The identity of a person requires physical immediacy as the reference point for reflection.

Reflexivity

If the notion of identity is understood as the self-reference of a person, the reflexivity of this reference is unavoidable. This is because the other side of physical immediacy is the indirect ascertainment of oneself. With respect to itself the subject is, accordingly, always too late. On the other hand, self-reflection enables us to take up a position of distance with respect to ourselves from which physical immediacy as such can be considered. In reflecting on ourselves, identity constitutes itself as a definite quantity capable of articulation. To perceive oneself as oneself and to refer to oneself is a capacity which distinguishes personal identity from every other identity which is assigned to us by others. It not only effects the identification of self over time, that is, the certainty that one is the same person today as yesterday; it also creates self-concepts which will concern us more precisely later.

Temporality and continuity

By means of the reflective character of identity, its reference to time can be defined in a number of different respects. On the one hand, identification with oneself takes place reflexively, so that it first becomes meaningful to speak of an 'identity' and not merely different states of being which e.g. just happen to bear a name that remains the same over time although everything else changes. On the other hand, the ascertainment of our own history occurs reflexively; indeed, a life story as such is constituted only by means of the reflexive combination of different episodes which follow each other in time. Identity requires a certain amount of continuity, which must ultimately outweigh the discontinuity, even when a person moves between the two poles. The temporal form of personal identity is lived and experienced life history. In this respect, one must distinguish between objective time, for example, a person's lifetime and the historical events which occurred during it, and subjective time, which refers not only to the personal events and experiences of a life but also to its subjectively experienced duration. An example of this is the way in which traumatic experiences can remain constantly present for someone and so do not pale into memory and become part of that person's biography as an episode which is remembered but belongs clearly to the past. Often it is precisely the traumatic experiences or at least the distressing ones which necessitate a new interpretation of one's own identity or biography.

Dialogicity and intersubjectivity

Identity is won through and in conflict with the identities others ascribe to us. This begins with the simple fact that persons speak about themselves and in doing so make use of a language convention which has been taken over from their primary significant others. In self-reflection, for example, we use the name that other people have given us. A name is not chosen autonomously; rather, it is taken over and at the most filled with individual meaning in the course of the development of identity. It is often the case that with the help of a name a continuity between generations is created which is in turn intended as a source of identity. In the tradition of G. H. Mead, however, the dialogical constitution of identity implies even more. Mead created the concepts 'I' and 'me' in order to express two different dimensions of personal identity. The 'I' perspective indicates the individual self-perspective which I have just divided further into physical and reflective dimensions. The 'me' perspective, on the other hand, is the perspective from outside, as it were, the way I experience it from others or rather in an act of imaginative sympathy can imagine it. What we are and who we are is often the result of an overwhelming force of external attributions and only to a small extent the success of our individual search for identity. Beyond this, the notion of identity proves in its dialogicity to be a dynamic concept, so that it is possible to speak of learning experiences and corrections in self-reference.

Contextuality

Individual identity or life history cannot be considered independently of the history of other people and the history of a given social context. Rather, a person's identity emerges from the interrelationship between context and integration on the one hand and individuality and differentiation on the other. To reflect on one's own identity without taking account of the context in which it is constructed leads to a reduced notion of identity, often even to serious misunderstandings of oneself. The relationship to a given socio-historical context and the differentiation or distancing of oneself from particular elements of meaning connoted by that context are therefore also constitutive parts of the concept of identity.

Individuality

Identity can only exist when a person is capable of being distinguished from other persons or objects. With reference to a person's identity, this means that the someone is 'particular' in the sense that he is different from other persons and that this difference is significant. Identity is constituted in the first place by means of uniqueness and irreplaceability, which in turn entails the need to be in harmony with oneself. This means that, as I said at the beginning, the notion of identity also involves a particular self-conception which contains the attitudes and convictions a person develops in the course of constructing an identity. At the same time, individuality resists every attempt to tie a person down to a certain identity, in that the particular cannot ultimately be captured in terms of fixed categories.

Narrativity

Although physical self-experience is immediate and individuality stands for uniqueness and incalculability, the identity of a person is dependent on articulation. The process of reflection takes place in the form of the telling of a life history; here, this latter notion becomes ambiguous, just as in another sense 'history' denotes not only an event but also the record of that event. It is no accident that time and record are joined in the concept of a life history, for the only appropriate articulatory form of the dialectic between objective time and the subjective sense of time is the telling of a story, which describes events and processes from the perspective of the subjects of the action and in this way constitutes the history of the protagonists as a story which can be told. The identity of a person grows out of the story she tells, revises and varies under the impression of new experiences.

2. *Narrative identity as bridge between description and prescription*

In the following, the role of narrativity is developed further. The telling of a life story, as we have seen, is the narrative form of framing and at the same time constituting a person's identity. By narrating a life, a person gains the contours which are appropriate to the duration, individuality and physical mediation of experience. The narrative proceeds according to specific evaluative points of view, which are dependent on the perspective of the narration, that is to say, of the present, whenever that may happen to be.

Does it not, however, make a considerable difference whether I take everyday story telling as my starting point or literary narration? Doesn't one have to take into account the fact that the point of reference of one's own life story is that which one has really experienced, and that the narration to that extent wants to be 'authentic', whereas a literary biography can be fictional or authentic and is to that extent 'autonomous' in its relationship to reality? This is quite true, but has not always been adequately taken into account – Alasdair MacIntyre, for example, ignores this point completely, and even Michel Foucault underestimates it in his theory of aesthetic existence. Martin Seel on the other hand denies the difference between existence or rather between ethics and aesthetics when he tries to make art into a component of the ethics of the good life. My concern at the moment, however, is rather a definition of the connection between existence and aesthetics. For this, not only the connection but also the difference between actions, practices and 'life' in general on the one hand and 'story telling' of the kind which takes place in literature on the other must be clarifed. Here Paul Ricoeur's sophisticated notion of mimesis is important. Ricoeur distinguishes between three levels of mimesis, which also become relevant for the conception of narrative identity. Mimesis II, the configuration in narration, is framed by prefiguration in praxis (mimesis I) and refiguration in reception (mimesis III), which are themselves forms of mimesis. The theory of mimesis composed of three elements assumes that one can say that as soon as praxis is understood as such, it is narratively or prenarratively structured, and that the act of the reception of stories demands in turn an activity which can be identified as mimesis.

One can deduce the prefiguration of narration in praxis, mimesis I, because different skills are required in telling and understanding stories which are gained in the praxis. This is first of all the competence to understand actions as such; second, the competence to understand symbolic mediation. The content is not directly communicated, but is rather bound to the intersubjective process of giving meaning to specific symbols. Language consists of a complex of symbols which constructs the context of all actions. Symbols structure and introduce value judgments which with reference to actions take on an ethical quality. Third, stories assume the competence to recognize the temporal structures of actions which run through the praxis.

The prefiguration of narration in the praxis supplies the telling of stories with a horizon which consists in the competence of the semantic, symbolic and temporal understanding of human action. In this respect, therefore, prefiguration means that structural elements which are already present in the praxis recur in the story, and that the praxis is quasi-narratively or prenarratively structured by means of significance. The story, considered as the active shaping of reality in the form of a literary text, is bound by means of this pre-understanding to extra-literary reality; literature is distinguishable in its distance from significant reality, but not removable.

The distance to prefigured reality which enters into the story is the concern of the configuration of the narrative, which Ricoeur calls mimesis II. The narrative takes up aspects of reality and passes them on by way of a new creation. It therefore stands between tradition and radical new creation, connected with reality through pre-understanding and the rules of composition which it takes up and develops further, but also connected with that reality which is the future and can only become a new present in the act of reception. Narration in the sense of mimesis II can proceed historiographically, that is, authentically, or fictionally, that is, autonomously in its relationship to reality. Both styles of narration have common elements in their relationship to time, but prove to have considerable differences in the way in which they shape reality. Ricoeur calls the relationship between the two 'crossed reference': a literary narrative cannot free itself entirely from experienced and experienceable reality; non-fictional narrative, however, creates a unity, chooses aspects worth telling, etc., which sometimes bring it very close to literature.

In the act of reading, mimesis III, the narrated story is actualized. Reception is also based on schematization and tradition. The reader comes to the story with particular expectations which can be described as the implicit knowledge of rules. She is confirmed in her understanding by means of the rules which are realized in the narrative and perceives departures from the rules. To this extent the act of reading is the 'operator' between mimesis II and mimesis III.

In reception, the world of the text and the world of the reader overlap. The narrative refers according to Ricoeur to a 'world' which is to be considered as the other of the text, which, however, is expressed in the narration and by means of the narration. The literary text expresses experiences from the non-literary reality, nevertheless in the modus of the possible. To that extent, that 'which is interpreted in a text is the suggestion of a world in which I live and which could create my most personal possibilities'.[1]

Not only do stories in general articulate ethical convictions and ethically relevant experiences, but also and especially life stories as the expression of a person's self-identity. At this point, therefore, I come to my second guiding question, that is, the question of the meaning of the notion 'moral identity'. I follow again in the wake of Paul Ricoeur, who deals with the same question in *Oneself as Another*.

II. Moral identity: Paul Ricoeur's approach

Ricoeur sees a close connection between evaluations with respect to goods or goals which are pursued in actions and a person's self-affirmation. My sense of self-worth is not called into question by every evaluation, but rather particularly by those which concern the core of my identity. It is therefore the sense of self-worth which moves the concern with the good life into the area of ethics.

Second, the individual lifestyle is nevertheless bound to contexts and intersubjective involvements. The pursuit of the good life therefore entails more than just the sense of self-worth that a person needs. It also involves goodwill towards others, the desire to live 'well' with others. With this realization, Ricoeur takes up a tradition of ethics which was long forgotten because it is based on emotions and appeared incapable of being rigorously argued. However, as Ricoeur says, goodwill towards others, solicitude, is a central aspect of our ethical involvement with others. The Christian word for 'solicitude' is love, particularly understood in a charitable sense; the ethical principle which gives it its normative content is the Golden Rule, which also has an outstanding status in Christian ethics. In the language of modernity, solicitude consists in care for another and others, who in this way become a factor in my action. Ricoeur grounds it as a spontaneous impulse in the pursuit of the good life. A good model for this is friendship, in which we experience respect for another person as something we want to show and precisely not as something we ought to show, in the way that morality will demand it. The request or wish that you respect me the way that I respect you, or your request to me that I do not hurt you and instead encourage and support you in your pursuit of a good life, takes precedence over the command or imperative of morality.

Since our involvement with others does not consist entirely of inter-personal relationships, there will need to be institutions and structures which allow us free and benevolent dealings with each other. To this extent, a sense of justice, understood in the Aristotelian sense as a virtue, to establish institutions with reference to the equality of its members, belongs to the pursuit of the good life. A sense of justice is therefore the basis of all more-than-individual relationships and structures.

There is nevertheless a fracture which runs through the pursuit of the good life. The freedom of human action makes possible not only spontaneous good, but also and to exactly the same extent hate and violence towards others. The fact that the major theoreticians of moral sensibility –

Shaftesbury, Hutcheson and even Hume – allowed this aspect to go by the board or at least to remain unaddressed led to Kant's merciless criticism of their 'aesthetic naïveté' (*Schöngeisterei*). Kant's categorical imperative can be understood only with reference to the potential for violence inherent in human action; only with respect to this background is the moral 'ought' meaningful. Because of the possibility of violence in action, and because there is such as thing as an 'inclination towards evil', a destructive tendency in human nature, it is not enough to rely on the pursuit of the good. As Ricoeur puts it:

> Because there is evil, the aim of the 'good life' has to be submitted to the test of moral obligation, which might be described in the following terms: 'Act solely in accordance with the maxim by which you can wish at the same time that what *ought not to be*, namely evil, will indeed *not exist*' (*Oneself as Another*, 218).

Evil is first of all described as the disregard of moral autonomy in Kant's sense, who used this notion to describe a person's capacity for morality. To deny one's responsibility for one's own life and actions, to remain in a position of dependency and disenfranchisement when there are alternatives, to refuse to be or become a moral subject: this not merely contradicts the conditions of self-worth on the level of ethical striving; it is much more disregard of one's self. Respect for the self is accordingly morally right as respect for an authority which has to give itself the moral laws. The first part of the content of Ricoeur's imperative could then run as follows: act according to the maxim which means that you can at the same time desire that that which should not be, is not: the disregard of your own self.

In the second part, solicitude is translated into respect for other people. Even at the point at which I lose an emotional reason to encounter another person with goodwill, I am morally obliged to respect him or her as a person. In its second part, therefore, Ricoeur's imperative could run: act according to the maxim which means that you can at the same time desire that that which should not be, is not: the disregard of another person.

In the third part, the sense of justice is translated into a principle of justice which is grounded on a level which transcends the individual. Here e.g. Rawls' theory of justice can be brought in, and the differentiation carried out by Michael Walzer as well. Accordingly, the third part of Ricoeur's imperative could run: act according to the maxim which means that you can at the same time desire that that which should not be, is not: the establishment of unjust structures.

This newly formulated moral imperative for the stemming of evil is, how-ever, too formal to be able to be directly useful for the practice of shaping one's life or establishing institutions. In addition, it paints in black and white, whereas in practice it is often the case that only shades of grey and borderline cases are to be found.

For this reason it seems sensible to assume a relationship of complement-arity between the ethics of the good life and morality, although here Ricoeur assigns the foundational power to the ethics of the good life:

> What makes conviction an inescapable party here is the fact that it expresses the positions from which result the meanings, interpretations, and evaluations relating to the multiple goods that occupy the scale of praxis, from practices and their immanent goods, passing by way of life plans, life histories, and including the conceptions humans have, alone or together, of what a complete life would be. For, finally, what do we dis-cuss, even on the level of political practice, where the goods concerned transcend the goods immanent in various practices – for example, in the debate of the ends of good government of the legitimacy of democracy – yes, what do we discuss, if not the best way for each party in the great debate to aim, beyond institutional mediations, at a complete life with and for others in just institutions? The articulations that we never cease to reinforce between deontology and teleology finds its highest – and most fragile – expression in the *reflective equilibrium between the ethics of argu-mentation and considered convictions* (*Oneself as Another*, 288f.).

On the basis of this 'little ethics' (*Oneself as Another*, 290), Ricoeur is now able to create an appropriate notion of moral identity. The ascription of an action to an agent now proceeds according to the notion of ethical and moral accountability. This accountability has, in a way, two sides: with respect to the identification of a self imputability is the central term. With respect to the concept of a self, however, responsibility becomes central. In both cases, however, the connection between narrative and moral identity is created by means of the adoption of the concept of time. It is not the agreement or rather proximity or distance to a good in general which is the criterion for successful identity – as is the case in Taylor's approach – but rather the taking on of responsibility: responsibility for the consequences of an action as responsibility with respect to the future, responsibility for the past 'which affects us without its being entirely our work but what we take on as ours' (*Oneself as Another*, 293), and responsibility in the present.

Accordingly, moral identity is the identity which answers for itself and its actions in its temporal entanglement and accordingly articulates them in its life story. The unity of identity in time which was provided on the level of narrative identity by the unity of the story is accordingly achieved on the level of moral identity by the taking of responsibility for the past, the present and the future and its integration in the life story. Inasmuch as moral identity is based on narrative identity, however, the relationship between ethics and aesthetics is defined as well. Only moral identity is capable of distinguishing the 'seriousness' of existential life from the 'game' of the aesthetic life story or of fiction. Every attempt to resolve ethical existence into an aesthetic existence is doomed to failure because of the necessity of taking on responsibility. Ricoeur has succeeded in showing this and, beyond this, in anchoring the possibility of responsibility in a 'hermeneutics of the self'.

Note

1.   W. Schapp, *In Geschichten verstrickt*, 127.

Bibliography

Michel Foucault, *History of Sexuality*, Vol. 3: *The Care of the Self*, Harmondsworth 1990
Hille Haker, *Moralische Identität. Literarische Lebensgeschichten als Medium ethischer Reflexion. Mit einer Interpretation der Jahrestage von Uwe Johnson*, Tübingen 1999
A. MacIntyre, *After Virtue. A Study in Moral Theory*, London and Notre Dame 1981
P. Ricoeur, *Oneself as Another*, Chicago 1992
——, *Time and Narrative* (3 vols), Chicago 1985
M. Seel, *Ethisch-Ästhetische Studien*, Frankfurt am Main 1996
C. Taylor, *Sources of the Self. The Making of Modern Identity*, Cambridge 1989
——, 'Was ist menschliches Handeln', in *Negative Freiheit. Zur Kritik des neuzeitlichen Individualismus*, Frankfurt am Main 1988, 9–51

Virtue and Identity

Introduction

In this article, I first examine the interplay between virtues and an anthropological vision of human identity. Then, I propose cardinal virtues for an adequate expression of the contemporary anthropological vision.

I. The interplay between virtues and an anthropological vision of human identity

The virtues are traditional heuristic guides that collectively aim for the right realization of human identity. The virtues are heuristic, because in their nature they are teleological. As teleological, they need to be continually realized and redefined; their final definition remains outstanding. Their nature is, then, historically dynamic; being in themselves goal-orientated, they resist classicist constructions but rather require continually to be understood, acquired, developed and reformulated.

The historical dynamism of the virtues applies correspondingly to the anthropological vision of human identity which guides us in our pursuit of the virtues. That vision is also, in its nature, historically dynamic. As we grasp better who each and every human person can become, to that extent we need to reformulate the virtues. As we determine our anthropological vision, we subsequently designate corresponding virtues to fill in or 'thicken' the image of the human that we aim at.

Thus, Aristotle's elitism led him to discuss virtues primarily for those who could be magnificent. While he designated other virtues for educated men, he did not develop any for women or slaves. But as philosophers and theologians further developed a more inclusive anthropology, they needed virtues that substantiated this democratic framework.

The dialectical interplay between these historically dynamic concepts of the anthropological vision of human identity and the corresponding human virtues can be seen from a variety of viewpoints. Years ago in *Concilium*, Dietmar Mieth, for instance, outlined the changes of value among historical and economic societies and described the prototype of each society in terms of its prototypical virtuous person.[1] Likewise, Clodovis Boff proposed a set of virtues that pointed heuristically toward a liberating anthropology for the poor.[2]

1. The task of moral theologians

Underlying the teleological nature of the virtues is, then, an implicit belief in the progress of ethical thought. For instance, in that same collection, Anne Patrick described how the historical narrative of a particular person as proto-typically virtuous can be seen in hindsight as oppressive. In her article she examined the canonization of Maria Goretti and suggested that it implicitly proposed a woman's chastity as a social virtue of greater importance than a woman's own life.[3] Patrick presumed an ethically objective progression in our insights in the shift from a classical patriarchal anthropology in which chastity was the signature virtue for women to a more egalitarian, liberation anthropology where justice was the hallmark virtue for both genders.

Patrick's progress is not simply descriptive, but rather normative. Progress in articulating and proposing both an anthropological vision and the corresponding virtues doesn't just happen; ethicists and moralists have the quadruple task of critically reflecting on the contemporary situation to see whether existing anthropologies and the corresponding constellations of virtues inhibit or liberate members of our global community, perceiving new horizons of human possibility, expressing the possible ways that virtue can attain those horizons, and making politically possible the actual new self-understanding and self-realization. This final task is often overlooked: too often ethicists and moralists think that our work ends with written pro-posals, but inasmuch as ethical insight, *to be ethical,* must end in action, similarly the task of the ethicist must end in political action, an insight that Aristotle routinely affirmed.

Like philosophers and theologians before and after him, Josef Fuchs rightly affirmed that the task of the ethicist and moral theologian is therefore to promote actively the progress of humanity.[4] This task became known as liberation theology, which intentionally developed a specifically, historically progressive theological task of promoting the good of all human beings, see-ing the option for the poor as the guarantor for an inclusive anthropological horizon.[5] This theology resulted from a re-examination of current christology, ecclesiology and eschatology and argued, as I have above, that the end of theology is praxis. In the light of this re-examination and its new dialectical method they also insisted that the task of the moral theologian was critically and practically to advance both an anthropological vision and corresponding virtues.[6]

More recently, European moral theologians have developed these insights by revising our understanding of the relationship between the natural law and salvation history. In this way, they complemented the historical revisionism done by the liberation theologians and proposed that the *humanum* of the natural law had to be as historically dynamic and open to reformulation as was the *Christus* upon which the *humanum* is based.[7]

These theologians are not abandoning a universal accessibility to the natural law by sequestering it into a sectarian or theistic camp. Natural law is the universally accessible study through human reason of a normative anthropology. But we each perceive the natural law from our own context as Karl Mannheim taught us. Christian ethicists perceive the *humanum* with the eyes of faith. This does not mean, then, that they are claiming that moral prescriptions are deduced from truths of faith. Rather, they believe that their perception will be prompted by a particular urgency because of the narrative of salvation history. Instead of talking about new essential norms, as Klaus Demmer puts it simply: 'genuine theology leads to a fundamental change in our way of thinking'.[8]

Our hermeneutical investigations into the nature of human identity, the horizon of our anthropological vision and the corresponding virtues are not relativistic but dependent on history. Because they depend on history, our hermeneutic investigations are not circular. As Thomas Kopfensteiner points out, because we are operating from an historical viewpoint as opposed to a classicist one, we see human history progressing. The 'shape' of our hermeneutics is not a closed circle, therefore, but an open spiral moving forward.[9]

2. *The historical perspective of moral theologians*

The appropriateness of a particular virtue is ascertained by the articulation of our anthropological vision. Sometimes, whether or not a particular virtue aims to advance our vision depends not on the virtue itself but rather on its relationship to the constellation of other virtues. For instance, in the article by Patrick, by itself chastity is an important virtue, but the priority of place it received in the patriarchal description of the virtuous woman does not make it, in that case, an effective tool for the right realization of women. In a similar way, Karen Lebaqcz and Shirley Macemon recently raised the case of pastors who notoriously underpay their staff, claiming that their employees must be 'patient'. The authors argued that patience is an auxiliary virtue of justice and if there is no justice, then patience is a vice.[10]

Particular virtues can be as underestimated as they are overestimated. Patricia Beattie Jung rightly complains that proponents of virtue have so overlooked the passions that their corresponding virtues are usually designated to control and inhibit, and not to engage and promote the passions.[11]

A dialectic emerges. As we further determine our anthropological vision, to that extent we further amend or reformulate our virtues. But it is a full dialect in that we cannot further determine our anthropological vision without actually appropriating the virtues that help us to have a fresh perspective on humanity. Again, as Karl Mannheim taught us, our knowledge depends on our perspective.

Virtue ethicists make an important caveat to Mannheim's claim. Only the person of good character enjoys an adequate perception. Mannheim's claims are rooted in, yet amplified by Aristotle. As Aristotle writes:

> For the man of good character judges every situation rightly; i.e., in every situation what appears to him is the truth. Every disposition has its own appreciation of what is fine and pleasant; and probably what makes the man of good character stand out furthest is the fact that he sees the truth in every kind of situation: he is a sort of standard and yardstick.[12]

We should not read Aristotle from a classicist perspective, however. Rather, there is a historical interplay between the state of our character and our ability to see. Each informs the other. Our ability to perceive depends upon our character, but we cannot develop that character rightly until we rightly perceive. This dialectically dependent development is the foundation of the dynamism within virtue ethics.

Most virtue ethicists believe that the right realization of persons is not a construct but depends upon our discovering a correct anthropology of human identity. Martha Nussbaum, for instance, refuted the claim of relativism and noted that Aristotle offered an objectively rational mean for the eleven spheres of life that all persons experienced.[13] Comprehensively, those spheres provided a sketch of Aristotle's anthropology.

The claim of moral objectivity is not then negated by the recognition of our historical context. But our right perception of that mean or what we today would call the anthropological goal of a particular character trait depends upon our ability to perceive it in the first place. This is why Aristotle recommended to us that we find the mean by seeing how a prudent person would determine it.[14]

Yet Aristotle departed from Socrates on the point that prudence is sufficient for self-realization and self-determination. Prudence, Aristotle warned us, depended upon the other virtues, and those virtues were dialectally dependent upon prudence.[15] For this reason, the competency of prudence is deeply imbedded in the historicity of human beings such that human beings can only perceive well the horizon of their possibilities to the extent that they have rightly realized themselves through the virtues.[16]

II. Realizing the agenda for human identity

In the current retrieval of virtue ethics, we need to go further than simply examining particular virtues to develop human identity. We need to examine a constellation of virtues, in particular, the cardinal virtues. The name 'cardinal' suggests that all other virtues 'hinge' on these four and, therefore, as such they sculpt the outline of our anthropological vision.

If we take the cardinal virtues as they are proposed in Thomas Aquinas, who built upon the insights of Cicero, Ambrose, Gregory and Augustine, we find that the four cardinal virtues – prudence, justice, temperance and fortitude – perfect four corresponding powers: the practical reason, the will, the concupiscible, and the irascible. These virtues inhere in a particular hierarchy. Temperance and fortitude are predominantly at the service of justice. Prudence determines the right choice of means for each of the virtues, but it especially looks to recommend the just action, since justice governs all exterior principles. In a manner of speaking, the anthropological identity of the virtuous person is simply the just one.

These virtues and their over-arching structure are, however, no longer adequate and in fact endorse an anthropology that inhibits greatly the present theological agenda. As far as I see it, three reasons merit replacing them. First, contemporary writers repeatedly express dissatisfaction with the insufficiency of justice. For the most part, they offer hyphenated constructs, the most famous being 'love-justice', which attempts to acknowledge that while working for the equality for all persons, we still maintain partial relationships that need to be nurtured and sustained.[17]

But the hyphen is distracting. Rather than reducing one to the other or eliding the two together, Paul Ricoeur places them in a 'tension between two

distinct and sometimes opposed claims'.[18] Ricoeur's insight that the virtues
are distinct and at times opposing stands in contrast with Aquinas' strategy
of the cardinal virtues, where justice is supported by fortitude and temperance and neither shaped nor opposed by the two auxiliary virtues. Only
when another virtue stands as a fully equal heuristic guide can there be
a dialectical tension wherein the virtues challenge and define one another
and, as Ricoeur suggests, 'may even be the occasion for the invention of
responsible forms of behaviour'.[19]

Second, the modern era insists that moral dilemmas are not based on the
simple opposition of good and evil but, more frequently, on the clash of
goods. Thus, a constellation of heuristic guides that already resolves the
priority of one virtue over another by a preconceived hierarchal structure
pre-empts realism. We cannot propose heuristic guides that prefabricate
solutions when the concrete data are still forthcoming.

Third, the primary identity of being human is not an individual with
powers needing perfection, but rather a relational rational being whose
modes of relationality need to be realized rightly. Moreover, this latter
description is much more conducive to providing a context for cross-
cultural discussion than one that describes the virtues as the perfection of
particular powers.

Our identity is relational in three ways: generally, specifically and uniquely. Each of these relational ways of being demands a cardinal virtue: as a
relational being in general, we are called to justice; as a relational being
specifically, we are called to fidelity; as a relational being uniquely, we
are called to self-care. These three virtues are cardinal. Unlike Thomas'
structure, none is ethically prior to the other; they have equally urgent
claims and they should be pursued as ends in themselves: we are not called
to be faithful and self-caring in order to be just, nor are we called to be self-
caring and just in order to be faithful. None is auxiliary to the others. They
are distinctive virtues with none being a sub-set or sub-category of the other.
They are cardinal. The fourth cardinal virtue is prudence, which determines
what constitutes the just, faithful and self-caring way of life for an individual.

Our relationality generally is always directed by an ordered appreciation
for the common good in which we treat all people as equal. As members
of the human race, we are expected to respond to all members in general
equally and impartially.[20]

If justice urges us to treat all people equally, then fidelity makes distinc-
tively different claims. Fidelity is the virtue that nurtures and sustains the

bonds of those special relationships that humans enjoy whether by blood, marriage, love, citizenship or sacrament. If justice rests on impartiality and universality, then fidelity rests on partiality and particularity.

Fidelity here is like love in the 'just-love' dialectic. It is also like the claim that Carol Gilligan made in her important work, *In a Different Voice*.[21] Gilligan criticized Lawrence Kohlberg for arguing that full moral development was found in the person who could reason well about justice as impartial and universal. She countered that the human must aim both for the impartiality of justice as well as the development of particular bonds.

Neither of these virtues, however, addresses the unique relationship that each person has with herself or himself. Care for self enjoys a considered role in our tradition, as for instance the command to love God and one's neighbour as oneself. In his writings on the order of charity, Thomas Aquinas, among others, developed this love at length.[22]

Finally, prudence has the task of integrating the three virtues into our relationships, just as it did when it was among the classical list of the cardinal virtues. Thus, prudence is always vigilant looking to the future, trying not only to realize the claims of justice, fidelity and self-care in the here and now, but also calling us to anticipate occasions when each of these virtues can be more fully acquired. In this way prudence is clearly a virtue that pursues ends and effectively establishes the moral agenda for the person growing in these virtues. But these ends are not in opposition to nor in isolation from another. Rather, prudence helps each virtue to shape its end as more inclusive of the other two.

Inasmuch as all persons in every culture are constituted by these three ways of being related, by naming these virtues as cardinal we have a device for talking cross-culturally. This device is based, however, on modest claims. The cardinal virtues do not purport to offer a picture of the ideal person, nor to exhaust the entire domain of virtue. Rather than being the last word on virtue, they are among the first words, stating the bare essentials for right human living and specific action. As hinges, the cardinal virtues provide a skeleton of both what human persons should basically be and at what human action should basically aim. All other issues of virtue hang on the skeletal structures of both rightly-integrated dispositions and right moral action.

Human identity is worked out in a variety of contexts, but virtue ethicists, in particular, have the task of elucidating that identity by providing practical guides. Sensitive to the fact that religious, cultural and personal communities are especially interested in thickening virtues, virtue ethicists offer these

guides only heuristically to help in furthering the historically progressive
task of expressing the human.

Notes

1. Dietmar Mieth, 'Continuity and Change in Value Orientations', in Dietmar
   Mieth and Jacques Pohier (eds), *Changing Values and Virtues, Concilium* 191,
   1987, 47–59.
2. Clodovis Boff, 'The Poor of Latin America and their New Ways of Liberation',
   ibid., 33–45.
3. Anne Patrick, 'Narrative and the Social Dynamics of Virtue,' ibid., 69–80.
4. Josef Fuchs, 'On the Theology of Human Progress', *Human Values and
   Christian Morality*, Dublin 1970, 178–203.
5. Ignacio Ellacuría and Jon Sobrino, *Mysterium Liberationis*, Maryknoll, NY
   1993.
6. For instance, Antonio Moser and Bernardino Leers, *Moral Theology: Dead
   Ends and Alternatives*, Maryknoll, NY 1990.
7. James F. Keenan and Thomas R. Kopfensteiner, 'Moral Theology out of
   Western Europe', *Theological Studies* 59, 1998, 107–35.
8. Klaus Demmer, 'Die autonome Moral – einige Anfrage an die Denkform', in
   Adrian Holderegger (ed.), *Fundamente der theologischen Ethik*, Freiburg 1996,
   261–76: 262.
9. See Thomas R. Kopfensteiner, 'The Metaphorical Structure of Normativity',
   Theological Studies 58, 1997, 331–46.
10. Karen Lebacqz and Shirley Macemon, 'Vicious Virtue? Patience, Justice and
    Salaries in the Church', in James F. Keenan and Joseph J. Kotva, Jr (eds),
    *Practice What You Preach: Virtues, Ethics and Power in the Lives of Church
    Ministers and Their Congregations*, Franklin, WI: Sheed and Ward 1999.
11. Patricia Beattie Jung, 'Sanctification: An Interpretation in Light of
    Embodiment', *Journal of Religious Ethics* 11, 1983, 75–94.
12. Aristotle, *Nichomachean Ethics*, Harmondsworth 1984, III, 1113a12–34.
13. Martha Nussbaum, 'Non-Relative Virtues: An Aristotelian Approach', in Peter
    A. French et al. (eds), *Midwest Studies in Philosophy 13, Ethical Theory:
    Character and Virtue*, Notre Dame 1988, 32–53.
14. Aristotle, *Nichomachean Ethics*, II. 1107a1–27.
15. Ibid., VI. 1144b10–1145a11.
16. Daniel Mark Nelson, *The Priority of Prudence: Virtue and the Natural Law in
    Thomas Aquinas and the Implications for Modern Ethics*, University Park, PA
    1992.
17. These are noted in my article, 'Proposing Cardinal Virtues', *Theological Studies*
    56, 1995, 709–29.
18. Paul Ricoeur, 'Love and Justice', in Werner G. Jeanrond and Jennifer L. Rike

(eds), *Radical Pluralism and Truth: David Tracy and the Hermeneutics of Religion*, New York 1991, 187–202: 196.

19. Ibid., 197.
20. Ibid., 195.
22. Carol Gilligan, *In a Different Voice: Psychological Theory and Women's Development*, Cambridge, Mass. 1982.
22. Stephen Pope, 'Expressive Individualism and True Self-Love: A Thomistic Perspective', *Journal of Religion* 71.3, 1991, 384–99; Vacek, *Love, Human and Divine*, 239–73.

A Critique of the Identity Paradigm

LUIZ CARLOS SUSIN

'War is the truth of being' (Heraclitus)

In the history of the West, identity can be seen as more than a first principle and a paradigm: it is an adventure and an uncertainty, but an adventure in quest of oneself and an uncertainty over satisfaction with oneself, both adventure and uncertainty questing for self-fulfilment and self-satisfaction as the identity of knowledge and of being. Can we see an extremely symptomatic confusion over identity in pre-Socratic thinking and even in Aristotle: does it concern a principle of the logical or the ontological order? Or does it involve both orders, of knowledge and of being itself?[1]

In truth, according to critics of this innocent beginning, it is a real reading key and a founding principle of Western history. This anxiety over identity can be seen at work behind heroic journeys in search of 'Eldorado' or the fountain of youth, behind the quest for and conquest of aesthetic and moral perfection, or even behind lines drawn to demarcate territories or institutions. Could identity be the great promise of happiness, purpose and the ultimate meaning of human existence, the lost paradise for which every human being longs?

Identity has been built up into an ideal model, a civilizing paradigm, a culture and a way of thinking. But we should perhaps observe, before stamping it as a Western paradigm, that we are possibly dealing with a drama of the whole human condition, which the West, beginning with the Greeks, has played out with the greatest pathos. Through the clarifying *logos*, the Greeks reflect back the word so that human beings can see themselves more sharply in the mirror of Narcissus that is typical of identity. It is not difficult, however, to find the question omnipresent in the whole vast Indo-European cultural area and even in other cultural regions. It is also not true to say that identity is the only paradigm present in the West, though it is its hegemonic paradigm, the victorious logic that overflows its history. Other logics that are not concerned with the paradigm of identity, that come into conflict with the triumphant logic of identity, have their own form of critical perseverance and resistance, which can be patient and long-lasting, within the womb of identity.

I. Identity as logical principle and theory

Identity is decisive in the construction of Western knowledge: it has been canonically erected into a first principle. It is this character of logical and theoretical 'principle' that crowns identity with an aura and a fascination that make it difficult to call into question. Emmanuel Lévinas, one of the main critics of identity, using the very logos that defines identity and, describing it exhaustively, has succeeded in clarifying the broad existential meaning and the quest for totality with which the identity movement has been pregnant from the beginning. It is not just a question of the simplest tautological statement – A is A – but a continuous process: 'A anxious for A or A enjoying A, always A held to A.'[2] Identity is, in effect, a process of identification. Just as Socrates is Socrates because 'Socrates socratizes', because every being is process, every noun is verb, so also, on principle, identity identifies, adaptation strives to adapt. We are dealing with an act or process, or rather – to use a musical metaphor that is perhaps the dominant tonality of Western music – it is a march, a great triumphal march, suited to armies on a strategic or ceremonial march. In logical terms, the process of identity is made up of a going out from oneself, a journey through difference, and a return to oneself, including all difference in oneself, crowning oneself as emphatic identity, in fullness, through the inclusion of difference in one's eschatological synthesis.

In the process of identification, anxious and tense identity on the way to the fullness of itself – A is A – contemplates, knows, conquers, concerns, appropriates, submits, digests, synthesizes all differences and even all otherness into itself: 'The circle of the Self encompasses or includes the circle of the Other.'[3] Only thus can it enjoy itself as full identity, in enjoying the triumph of this process of identification that embraces all differences. Otherwise, if it is impossible to submit and integrate itself, it proceeds by anathema, by excluding and demonizing difference. The Greeks' allergy to the *apeiron*, the indefinite or impossible to define, is symptomatic: it gives hints of the infinite and so unfinished, unperfected. This is intolerable for the identity project. The distinction is, in fact, one of the techniques of identification and appropriation, a well established technique in the process of understanding. In this sense, anathema would be recourse to distinction in order to clarify, understand and integrate better – in other words, a differentiation in the service of identification and of the totalization of identity. But that which cannot be reduced to identification when making this distinction can be regarded as barbarous or irreconcilably heretical, and efforts are made to eliminate it: the same process that identifies, that distinguishes in order to identify, also declares a just war.[4]

From pre-Socratics to moderns, the logos of identity has been built up into a basis, an understanding and a meaning. It has become established as wisdom and theoretical knowledge: it has raised itself to the stars of the firmament and looks down from a divine height, with the panoramic, all-embracing knowledge proper to a god. But it triumphs above all as critical understanding, distinguishing and identifying good and evil in a very particular way based on itself, on its glorious position as basis and referent of the whole of reality spread out at its feet. It has, then, become a detached and supposedly neutral sovereignty, like a prince laying down laws while hovering above them. This sovereign identity can really be the head of a prince, but it can equally be a city or a culture. In the West, however, the privilege of the *Cogito*, of the thinking and judging subject, conceptualizing and categorizing along the shelves of his subject, is one of the cleverest distinguishing secrets in the ambit of identification and identity. Its climax is the consciousness that is not only critical in relation to the things of its world but self-critical – self-analysing and self-identifying. It is as if consciousness were divided into itself and outside itself, into ingenuous and critical, into the conditions of impure and pure. In Hegel, this is the process of the 'spirit', the unfolding of reason, the great dialectic in which the identity of the identical and the non-identical obliges all difference to adjust itself and synthesize itself into the kingdom of identity. It is the necessary and logical sameness of the spirit in all difference.[5] In Descartes it is the human *Cogito* protected by God, but in Husserl it is simply the consciousness of the self, the selfhood in search of its transparency, its purity. In Freud it becomes an analytical method for the therapy of the self in its conquest of itself. But it can be a method for emphasizing and exhibiting self, the narcissistic spirituality of Western cultural post-modernity.

Writers on identity are numerous, but for present purposes Spinoza is most informative. The *conatus essendi* – striving to be – takes away from ontology but also from logic and theory, from knowledge and science, the aura of lightness and enchantment: the process of identity takes its place in a laborious self-realization and ontology, in a heroic perseverance, but one marked by tragedy, fatality, and struggle from its inception. Non-divine identity pays a high price in the process of identification and perseverance in its victories: there is waste, fatigue, and the need to persevere; there are threats and the need for vigilance: we cannot sleep; we must philosophize – even to the point of madness from excess of consciousness and saturating light, through a consciousness 'stuck' to the light, without shade in which to rest from itself. The sleepless identification of the *conatus essendi* – this striving to be inscribed on one's own self as a struggle for subsistence – mixed with the loneliness of day, the excess of light of the subject who reduces all others to his knowledge, and also the loneliness of night, in which the other arises in the shadows and disturbs the natural repose of identity in itself. Is not rising to the firmament of total theory, the ideal of identity, knowledge proper to a divinity, raising oneself tragically on Icarus' wings? Or is it necessary to bend oneself to the human limit, in which understanding is 'mere conjecture, always reformable',[6] the ephemeral knowledge of mortal creatures?

II. Identity as economics

Logical identity refers back to ontological identity and can then be narrated as history, as politics, and above all as economics. The process of identification does not just look enviously to the heights of light and theory. It seeks itself below, at the base, in the origin and within. Reduction or re-conduction to the foundation becomes an obsession of the process of identity in the field of ontology: it is at the foundation, at the *arche*, the base, that there lies not only the unbinding origin but the permanent secret of meaning and obligation. Unlocking the foundation, uncovering the *arche*, which involves methodical work of archaeological excavation, of measuring and comparing, is to lay identity bare and finally bring it to light, to set its realization more deeply in movement. The identity that clings to its foundation seeks not so much its eschatology as its protology, its origin. Now, the hard ground of reality is economic and ecological: it is mouth and bread, body and house – hearth and help – the soil itself and the hand that plants and reaps. Ontology begins by bringing together and identifying the verb 'to be' with the verbs 'to live', 'to eat', 'to work'. Those who can enjoy their identity are those who have good soup, a place to rest, hands to reap and also to make, to instrumentalize themselves, to 'gird themselves' and act to give shape to chaos, to define the indefinite, to take care of things, to reap fruits, all the while finding themselves once more, enriched by this work and this

adventure. Those who eat are the most just of people. And those who relax
in their houses are peaceful people.

In the ground, the foundation, the first thing found is not time but place.
There is, in the identity that rises up from itself as its basis and rests upon
itself, a priority of place and space over time and history. Only economic
insecurity leads to planning for tomorrow, to economic time-scaling and
conquest of place – of the whole world – through recourse to time. The
adventure of the history of the West can be regarded as the result of a
relatively successful economy that has joined time and history to space to
add different spaces to its identity in a colonized and globalized world. The
'superheating' of history and the compression of ages in modernity to the
detriment of spaces – history repressing and devastating geography, ecology
and the different cultures linked to different geographies – show an engulf-
ing history engaged in a gigantic effort at identity that conquers, despoils,
colonizes and globalizes every 'other' place. The ontology of the body, of
place, of a conscience founded on its 'own body' (in a phrase of Husserl's)
forces us to recognize an economy and an ecology at the root of ontology. In
this the Greeks were more conscientious than we moderns, knowing themselves to be 'shepherds of being' inserted into a cosmos, into a nature
of things that it was also proper to obey. Only in modern times have
Prometheus and other heroic figures become Cartesian or Faustian and
multiplied. More modestly, place and care for place are the beginning of
identity, even in one of the most celebrated concepts, that of person as a
hypostasis possessing logos, the attribute of the West.

The person as rational, thinking 'hypostasis', caring for oneself in a world
of objects and of life, but also as bodily hypostasis forming part of this world
of objects and of bodily life, is 'base', a 'basic position' (*hypo-stasis*, sub-
stance). Without this basic position no being would sub-sist. But, as Lévinas
has shown, the hypostasis has an existential dynamic by which it is
ontologically not something given but something formed in a dramatic
inaugural attitude of 'taking position', becoming an entity and an existent on
a sea of pure being or pure chaotic existence prior to the cosmos.[7] Being a
'subject', being a person, is to have succeeded in marking out a place to make
it into a reserved space, a protected inner place. Whether it is the skin of
one's body or the wall of one's house, this place coincides with the 'I', and it
is where the self arises as identity with a place, an own body, a consciousness
chez soi. This is why the person, the hypostasis, the identity, is private
property and a process of appropriation. Even when this hypostasis defines
itself as consciousness, differentiating itself and defining the confines of

itself like a clearing in the middle of a forest, this consciousness is an appropriation. What are said to be the 'character' or 'characteristics' of a person are in fact his or her 'properties', what is built up into an identity resting on these properties. What is most frightening about identity is that it subsists only as the stability of a property.

The juridical person, an extremely creative and decisive detail in the paradigm of identity as institution, as subject bearer of duties and rights, person 'bound by measures', is the most fascinating case of the working of the paradigm of identity, a Roman geniality by antonomasia. One of the modern consequences of this development of identity is that the freedom of each person ends where the freedom of the other begins. In other words, the act of freedom, the act *par excellence* that actuates the being itself of identity, however free it claims to be, has to remain circumscribed by the private property of identity. Relationships will be monadic, diplomatic, according to statutes and contracts that lend support to a portion of private properties and institutions in interaction within the dangerous contiguity of spaces in order to safeguard order and civilization, threatened by the chaotic violence of the spontaneity of freedom.

But the transgression of measures is inherent in the dynamism of the ever ongoing identification of identity. This is not only because each identity sets out from itself on a journey to what is different logically and gnoseologically, through understanding and accumulative knowledge. Understanding has a very close operative ontological ancestor – apprehension, the predation and assimilation of difference. Pascal saw this very clearly when he observed, '"There is my place in the sun." That is the origin and the image of the usurpation of the whole world.'[8]

III. Identity, hypostasis and karma

There are good indications of 'Indo-European' relationship between the Greek hypostasis and the Hindu karma.[9] Both concepts refer to a basic, stable reality, a platform on which all ontology is done. It is in the karmic condition that the avatars and reincarnations are inscribed, which, in Western terms, reside in the notions of metempsychosis and palingenesis. The notion of karma is based on the fatal appropriation of a reality, the reification and stability of life constituted in action, and the consequences created in the very act, which is tied into the karmic circle and develops it in new actions within a logic of cause and effect within which the effects become causes of new effects. The concept of karma, as at once both action and cause, has the advantage of describing the process of appropriation, the act of 'hypostasizing'. It is so resistant that it requires, coherently, a long and painful process of reincarnatory avatars for any change or improvement. That the belief in reincarnations and in atavistic 'returns' – the 'eternal return' – should be at least latent in the Western psyche is highly symptomatic. But the way of exercising it is diametrically opposed, for some obscure reason that has more to do with willed option than with the rational clarity proper to such choices and processes. For the Eastern Hindus, this karmic platform, the source of samsara, an almost infernal circle of reincarnations, calls for moksa, for the moment of liberation. The experience of moksa would be a liberation from identity imprisoned in its very sameness or even running the risk of worsening its condition in future returns. The very slow liberation is a work of ascesis, of retaliation against self and its processes of appropriation, since these processes are the karmic source of new imprisonments. Therefore, liberation is essentially a process of 'renouncing' – renouncing self in renouncing appropriation, depositioning and denuclearizing self, a movement of anti-identity.

There were plenty of ascetics among Platonists and the Greeks in general, such as the Stoics and especially the most radical, the Cynics. Modern existentialists, from Kierkegaard to Sartre, have also raised consciousness of the weight of things, of the body, even of conscience. In more religious terms, the Neoplatonists favoured the Christian mysticism of the desert anchorites. And the Franciscans and other movements embracing poverty in the Middle Ages had something of the Cynics or of Indian ascetics. But it was only in the East that this attitude became generalized as a widespread paradigm and stamped the culture. This is perhaps why the East is not so expansionist and destructive. In the West, on the other hand, the canons followed were not predominantly those of laying down and renunciation but those of realization and achievement, through processes of affirmation, appropriation, feudalism, conquest and expansion, in a spirit of optimism that modernity defined as evolution and progress. The reappearance of belief in reincarnation as found in Kardec's version of modern spiritualism keeps these Western connotations of identity in evolution, in more or less linear progress, where reincarnations themselves appear as new possibilities for identity, chances of reaching an identity desired as more extensive than that circumscribed by the temporal and local finitude of such a short life. The tragic realism of the Hindus, however, knows itself subject to the possibility of regression, imprisoned in the chains of a solid, solitary, exhaustingly workable identity.

The mediaeval discussions on property between the various religious movements and the pope are also very enlightening on the idea of identity as property. The most radical Franciscans, enamoured of total renunciation, applied the thesis of the 'naked Christ' in the individual and the community spheres, and this was bound to have consequences for the following of Jesus.[10] The papal reproval and later persecution and extinction of this most radical proposal in the church show the difficulty of a selfness *without identity* or, in other words, a naked and transparent authenticity without supports in any form of property and institution, without furthering oneself and affirming oneself as someone who conquers something in order to conquer oneself. Neither Hegelian identity nor even Marxist identity free themselves from the hard ground of property, of taking something over, something other, in order to take oneself over. If it is true that, as the Franciscan Spirituals said, God created an open world fit for angels and for God himself to walk in the evening breeze, and the devil – *diabolus*, precisely – created and crossed boundary walls, this is because he, the devil, is the father of lies and a murderer from the beginning (see John 8.44). The struggle for identity is the origin of war.

IV. War as truth of identity

Parodying Heraclitus, the father of dialectic, one can regard or even praise war and warriors as means of affirming identity. 'War is the truth of being': in the clash of opposites, what is remains, and what is not, or what was illusory, or what resists being, must turn from its appearance to not being, its natural destiny. But only the victors praise war and speak in defence of armed peace. It is in war, in the final analysis, that every *heteron* is drawn into the circle of the *auton*, even in the extreme form of annihilation. It is war that – cruelly – makes visible the processes of identification, of objectivization, of appropriation of every other to the point of imperial conquest.

The holy war waged by identity to reach itself coincides with the excellence of the 'One' and the passionate and messianic reduction of multiplicity to unity. But before the 'One', the unity and totality, became an ideal of ontology or metaphysics as reflected in Parmenides, Aristotle, or Plotinus, it was an experience learned and acclaimed in war. In the *Iliad*, Agamemnon succeeds in uniting the Greek cities against the Persians with the command 'Let one be the Lord'. Aristotle, at the end of chapter XII of his *Metaphysics*, transposes the Homeric expression to ontology: 'Existence refuses to be badly administered. The variety of powers is not good. Let one alone be Lord.'[11]

The passion for the One, the Platonic and above all Neoplatonic mysticism, clouding the trinitarian narrative of the Christian New Testament, is a key piece in the composition of Western identity. To the One are linked the invention and ennoblement of hierarchy as a strategy of submission to the totality, the efficacious relationship between the One and the All, the One embracing and coinciding with the All through the plot, emanating from or administered by the hierarchy, the nobler the closer it gets to the One, the more warrior the more it approximates to plurality in order to keep it in the totality.[12] An otherness, however foreign and strange it may appear beyond the horizon, remains referred to the totalizing identity of the One. But the moderns know that such power of identification and totalization does not come from a god. It can come from a Napoleon or a Hitler, from a dictatorial or imperialistic enterprise, the crowning of a paranoid dream of identity. Closer to home, it can operate in technology or the faceless global market.

There is a surprise to be derived from the pithy statement of indigenous Guaraní thought, from the heart of Latin America, on evil and the 'one', in one of their sacred stories, lamenting that their wish is for the land without evils and, nevertheless, their reality is the ugly land: 'Things in their totality are one. And, for us, who have not desired this, they are more.'[13] According to the commentary collected by an anthropologist who sought to understand such a melancholy saying, 'It is because the totality of the things that make up the world can be said according to the One and not according to the multiple that evil is inscribed on the surface of the world [. . .] we suffer the destiny of the weight of the One: evil is the One. Our existence is suffering, because it unfolds under the sign of the One. Come, then, happy times of the long eternal sleeps, the calm dwelling where being is no longer told according to the One.'[14]

One, in the final analysis, leads to lack of relationship and to loneliness, which inclines it to decadence and corruption. Only a relationship with the 'other than self' can save. The anthropologist student of Guaraní culture ventures into a confrontation with Western thought: 'Do we not recognize here, in effect, almost even in the precise terms used, the metaphysical thought that, from its most distant Greek origins, has inspired the history of the West? In both cases, thoughts of the One and the not-One, of Good and Evil. But the pre-Socratic sages said that Good is the One, while the Guaraní thinkers claim that the One is Evil.'[15]

The question of the One in the Western metaphysical tradition is somewhat more complicated. The passionate and mystical claim, even with recourse to absolute transcendence, that the One heads the totality of multiplicity, that universality is under the transcendent One, corresponds to a political need for a monistic and monotheistic empire if totalization is to be complete.[16] Nevertheless, after all the wars to reduce the other to the same, to bring all difference within the dominant kingdom of identity, when the triumph of the Identical and its rest as crowned warrior is being celebrated, there also resounds its requiem and the beginning of its corruption, a dialectic with no apparent exit, in which *thanatos* and *eros* appear as two faces of the same reality. This is also why in the West, despite its ontological optimism, being is identified with evil, a closed circle of inter-existents, the world as hatred and vanity, in which the very totalization of identity is an indication of breaking up.[17]

Can there be a beyond as a homeland for identity? Not in the form in which we currently discover the way of identity through processes of identification and sameness. One of the parables of the West – recurring in figures such as Marco Polo, Christopher Columbus, or Yuri Gagarin, the cosmonaut who flew through the stratosphere and did not see God – is the figure of Odysseus and his spectacular Odyssey. The West is an Odyssey, in which it includes the stars. Odysseus' journey is, from the beginning of Homer's narrative, a journey back, a nostalgia in search of its origin, of its original secret, its other half persisting deep down in the warrior – Penelope. Odysseus wanders through the multiplicity of worlds, through every kind of difference, but he knows himself to be immune and triumphant and, furthermore, laden with experience and glories, laden with differences. He plans his approach to his home in the guise of a beggar to finally – supreme glory! – surprise and triumph over those who are living in his own house and to be reunited with his Penelope in the welcome of her bed: he, glorious identity adorned with all differences; she, persevering submission in veiled otherness, the hidden condition for the possibility of the return of her husband-lord-owner. The Odyssey of the West, as Lévinas roundly declares, is not an authentic adventure, it is a closed circle around sameness. There is an Odyssey and an identity in a minor key in the figure of Narcissus, who is immersed alone in his passion for himself and is consumed in himself, a post-festum key to the postmodern consumerist condition.

The glory of the West is to have played out a possible paradigm of the human condition, but at what cost! This form of identity is devastating. The West has to save itself from it, and this, by its very logic, is impossible. It can come only from outside, from another, from a relationship and a plurality that break and invert the curved line of identity pointing toward the same.

V. The Abrahamic alteration of identity

The pseudo-adventure of Odysseus can be confronted with the wandering figure of Abraham, pilgrim on a journey with no return, either for him or for his son. Going out from his family, his homeland, his language, and even from his religion based on the balance of sacrifice, Abraham, and then Sarah after him, had their names changed for the sake of a promise: ancestor of a multitude. The visitation by God almighty and the angel of the Lord, the trauma and novelty of these visitations, make Abraham into a pilgrim to what is beyond any horizon, a traveller to the absolute and the eschatological, in a sense a fugitive exposed and vulnerable to the approach of others. The identity in which Abraham perseveres to the end is his faithfulness in listening to and obedience to the surprises of another who challenges him and alters him at every step. No longer being an identity *chez soi* or for-itself, Abraham opens himself as a refuge and advocate for many, even for Sodom and Gomorrah. To be a child of Abraham, as Paul clearly saw (see Rom. 4) is to be a child of a freedom supported on another, to be dispossessed and to live only by one's reference to another. Or, as Jesus suggests (see John 8.56), it is to keep oneself in hope and trust – the biblical form of identity – for the joy of the Day of the Lord.

There is an Abrahamic way of narrating history, politics, economics. There is an Abrahamic culture, aesthetic, way of thinking. Opposed to the privilege of Oedipus and the Greek heroes, there is an Abrahamic form of psychoanalysis and civilization: the good competition in which the other's life moves forward with a blessing in the place of power and as the very exercise of power. Abraham is a canon placed like a cradle and a reversal in the closed and impenitent system of identity. He is the possibility of a de-nucleated subjectivity, exalted to transcendence at each step in the direction of the other. If it were not a contradiction, one could glimpse in his adventure an 'open identity', a perseverance in conversion and continuous reform, whose only fixed point is the other. In his quality of 'canon', Abraham can be discerned and recognized in other histories and in other cultures, even in other religions, in 'many nations'. He is, everywhere, the model of another way of living.

Translated by Paul Burns

Notes

1. Cf. C. Pires, 'Princípio', 'Logos', in *Enc. Luso-Brasileira de Filosofia* 4, Lisbon 1992, 418–23.
2. E. Lévinas, *En découvrant l'existence avec Husserl et Heidegger*, Paris ³1974, 187. His critique of identity can be found principally in his broadest book, *Totalité et infini*, The Hague 1961, in the first part, 'The Same and the Other'. But his whole *oeuvre* is filled with this critical stance in relation to identity. This article follows paths opened up by this Hebrew-French thinker.
3. E. Lévinas, *De Dieu qui vient à l'idée*, Paris 1982, 176.
4. Cf. C. Chalier, *Figures du féminin*, Paris 1982, 146. The writer extends Lévinas' critique to gender relationships.
5. Hegel is situated within the Aristotelian confusion between the Spirit of God and the human spirit: *o theos . . . nous estin* (Metaphysics, XII, 7) can be translated, in the historical development of Western understanding, as 'God is spirit', but more probably as 'God is reason' – reasoning is divine and is our participation in the divine. Or else, through reasoning there is a process of mutual absorption and an identification – an identity! – between the divine and the human. The spirit or reason in its perfection would necessarily be what one thinks of oneself. Cf M. Welker, *Gottes Geist. Theologie des Heiligen Geist*, Neukirchen-Vluyn 1992.
6. Pires, 'Logos' (n.1), 423.
7. It can be enlightening to compare Lévinas' description with the emergence of the ordered human world according to René Girard. This marvel of the emergence of the being that hypostasizes itself in a reflexivity, in folding back on itself as on a space, separates itself from the rest that is outside it. In the same way, in Girard's central theory regarding the emergence of order from chaos, the solid base, the firm and hidden foundation on which the solid cosmos sailing over chaos is separated and built, is the concentration of shapeless and undifferentiated energies on a single point, that of the heroic victim and his sacrifice. So would the person be underpinned by the price of a heroic sacrifice, something or someone who, in becoming property and support, loses his own being?
8. Lévinas cites Pascal at the beginning of his book that, traumatically, proposes another destination for subjectivity: *Autrement qu'être ou au-delà de l'essence*, The Hague 1974, vi.
9. Cf. M. Messier, 'Palingénésie', in *Catholicisme hier, aujourd'hui, demain X*, Paris 1985, 467–73. M. Biardeau, 'Karman', *Encyclopedia Universalis* 13, Paris 1996, 272–3.
10. Cf. *Bullarium Fransciscanum* V, 233ff.
11. Cf. E. Peterson, *Der Monotheismus als politisches Problem*, Leipzig 1935; J. Moltmann, *The Trinity and the Kingdom of God*, London 1981.
12. On the mystical, philosophical, ecclesiastical and political origins and meta-

morphoses of hierarchy, see G. Lafont, *Imaginer l'église catholique*, Paris 1996, 16–48; Moltmann, *Trinity* (n.11), 207.

13. Cf. P. Clastres, *Le grand parler – mythes et chants sacrés des Indiens Guarani*, Paris 1974.

14. Ibid., 14–15.

15. Ibid., 15.

16. In the debate on political theology, whereas Carl Schmitt claimed in 1922 that the most fruitful concepts of modern doctrine on the state were secularized theological concepts, Erik Peterson took the opposite view in 1935, seeking to demonstrate that there is a monotheistic 'mirroring' that derives from a monistic and imperialistic politics. According to Peterson, a truly trinitarian theology can never lead to justification of a sovereign power. The new wave of political theology, with Metz and Moltmann, qualifies the relationship between both poles in terms of 'alliance' between a conception of God and a conception of political organization and practice, both monistic and trinitarian. Cf n. 10 above.

17. 'Being is without response . . . The question is the very manifestation of relationship with being. Being is essentially strange, and does violence to us. We suffer its suffocating pressure like the night, but it does not respond. This is the evil of being' (Lévinas, *De l'existence à l'existant*, Paris ²1978, 28). Lévinas describes this discomfort in being as an impossibility of containing ourselves in our own skin, an inadequacy. It is not a question of a sickness of being, being insufficiently healthy, or deficiency in being, but being itself is suffering and 'pain': *Mal d'être*, the pain that is called 'being'. Cf. also R. T. de Souza, *Totalidade e desagregação. Sobre as fronteiras do pensamento e suas alternativas*, Porto Alegre 1996.

III. Theological Discussion

The Narrative Identity of Christians according to the New Testament

AGUSTÍN DEL AGUA

I. The narrative nature of Christian faith

The narrative form of confessing faith throughout the New Testament does not simply follow a generalized trend in religious phenomenology but is a result of the narrative nature of the Christian message. An event is being confessed and communicated. Therefore, Christian faith can be truly understood only by telling a story, just as happens in any individual process of Christian faith: it is the interventions of God in their own lives (experienced as foundational) that allow believers to narrate themselves (narrative identity) in the key of salvation.

In fact, the narrative form of confessing faith in the New Testament is in continuity with the narrative faith of the Old Testament tradition. The fact that biblical personages confess their faith by telling stories and giving accounts is due to the 'historical' character of biblical faith itself. History lends content to faith, while faith gives meaning to history. So Israel proclaims its faith by recounting events it experiences and understands as revelation of God (see Deut. 26.5–9), because in the Bible revelation is presented not as communication of a-temporal realities 'but as the written testimony of a series of interventions through which God reveals himself in human history'.[1] Likewise, the Gospels, hymns, confessions of faith, and so on in the New Testament 'tell' the Jesus-event (his life and destiny) as the eschatological workings of God in history (his full revelation). It is a message with a clearly narrative expression.

Faithful to this narrative form of confessing faith, Israel recounts its history following its faith process, just as believers today re-read their history in the light of their own faith process. Furthermore, Israel's faith is nourished by and grows through its recounting of this story. To this end, the Bible was in effect written as a tale retold: it continually returns to its past in order to open a new horizon on the future. So what is known as the 'Yahwist tradition', which present literary criticism of the Pentateuch sees as possibly an editing process rather than as a document, recounts the origins in the light of God's promise made in favour of the Davidic dynasty and in that of prophetic preaching.[2] The composition of Deuteronomic history is an account related from the origins to the destruction of Jerusalem in the light of the crisis of the exile; surprisingly, it is a fresh source of unquenchable hope in the future. The Gospels themselves recount the life, message, deeds, passion and death of Jesus in the light of the dazzling experience of the resurrection and the coming of the Holy Spirit as well as from the later experiences of the different communities that underlie the various Gospel accounts.

In this process of faith tied to history, Israel identified itself as people of God only when, on the basis of foundational experiences (such as 'God brought Israel out of Egypt'), it understood its whole history from beginning to end in a unity of meaning (threading together events, experiences), thus allowing it to narrate itself as a faith project by which God made it the bearer of the future universal salvation of humankind. In the same way, the clarification of the Christian identity came about through the production of narrative resources. On the basis, above all, of the founding experience of the death and resurrection of Jesus as a salvific event (as in 'he died for our sins and was raised for our salvation'), the Christian community came to identify itself through narrative, in continuity of unity of meaning with the Old Testament, as the eschatological people of God (or *ekklesia*) and bearer of the universal mission, in fulfilment of the promises of the old alliance (see Matt. 13).

This narrative form of confessing faith is undoubtedly one of the most important aspects of the relationship that exists between the Old and New Testaments. The Old Testament inheritance of the narrative nature of faith, based on God's interventions in history, contributed to preventing the original Christianity from dissolving into the world of mystery cults and into a mysticism deprived of all reference to time, which belongs more properly to philosophical thought removed from the central historical event of the incarnation.

II. The lost and recovered dimension of biblical narrative identity

The narrative dimension of biblical faith, then, encouraged contemporary exegesis to recover the religious dimension of the biblical account. After a long eclipse, exegesis has recovered the biblical account as a vehicle of religious identity. The separation between empirical fact and narrated event is inherited from a conception of history derived from the Enlightenment and rationalism. That led to the application of the historical-critical method to study of the biblical narrative. This approach suffered from the historicist epistemological presupposition that the events of history, if they were to be studied adequately, had to be separated from the interpretation made of them later. The consequence was that the biblical account lost its religious value in its historical dimension. Today, however, now that this lost dimension of the biblical narrative has been recovered, exegesis is very conscious that the narrators of the New Testament were not claiming to tell the 'story' of Jesus as ordinary neutral witnesses but to make it an authentic testimony of faith in God's action in it. This leads their narration to have the character of a proclamation or *kerygma* of salvation. The historical truth and the theological truth of the Jesus event both belong equally, then, to the account as two functions or dimensions inseparable from it. This is the narrative nature of the Christian faith, which can be manifested adequately only through being told.

Once the story had been recovered, the method of 'narrative analysis' contributed to mark it out as a form of religious identity. So 'telling of Jesus Christ' in the Gospels is not an abstract demonstration but the narration of the truth of a life that has to be handed on as the coming about of the experience of faith. On the basis of this experience, the saving character of the person and life of Jesus is expressed by the evangelists through recourse to the text and tradition already established as sacred. Thus the Christians, once they experienced the raising of Jesus brought about by God, saw in the concept of resurrection, developed by the Jews in the centuries immediately preceding the Christian era, the means of proclaiming such an event as the *kerygma* of salvation. Faith, however, does not depend on recourse to scripture. All Christian exegesis of the Old Testament starts from the prior confession that Jesus is the Lord, a confession of faith not arrived at by any exegetical deduction. This means that the semantic change the Christians introduced into the Old Testament traditions does not derive from yet another merely neutral interpretation of the Old Testament but from faith in

Christ, with all that implies for the hermeneutics of a Christian reading of the Old Testament.

The account, then, deals with events not on their historical surface but in their deep religious significance. Narrating means proclaiming faith in the Christ event as the eschatological working of God. A historical report could never tell how in Jesus' death the Old Testament reached its fulfilment (cf. John 19.30). It is the union between experience in faith and recourse to the Old Testament that gave rise to the Christian account. Accepting this, the type of narrative particular to the Gospels can then be qualified as 'interpretative account', 'narrative christology', 'christological discourse narrated as history', 'narrative kerygma', and so on. Put another way, we are dealing with an account in which exegesis and theology are not superimposed on the text but functions of the text itself. This means that the surface of the account covers a meaning that depends on hidden allusion to a repertory of texts from the Old Testament.

An immediate consequence of nascent Christianity seeing itself situated within the current of Jewish tradition was that the Easter faith postulated recourse to scripture as the only valid mode of presentation and justification to other Jews. Taking scripture as a whole, Christianity expressed in the only form possible that Jesus' course had developed according to God's plan, 'in accordance with the scriptures' (see 1 Cor. 15.3–4). From this postulate of the Easter faith it derived the principle that established the purpose and meaning of the Old Testament: the meaning of the Old Testament is Christ, and its purpose is to make his own mystery intelligible (see Luke 24.27). This semantic shift introduced by the Christians into the Old Testament is what constitutes the originality of the Christian background, the peculiarity of which lies in its being behind the 'fulfilment', since it starts from the source event of Christ and refers back to the Old Testament to explain it and confirm it.[3]

'Christian narrative identity' then shows that the New Testament experience of faith, in syntony with biblical faith, is inseparable both from the event from which it stems and from the *kerygma* that expresses and proclaims it. It is therefore now clear that the great fault of 'kerygmatic theology' is to have sought to relate faith only to the *kerygma*, while maintaining that an 'account' is basically a form of illustrating the *kerygma*, but one that can also be rejected. The account shows, however, that the Christian experience of faith that stems from the historical existence of Jesus is inseparable from its mode of proclamation. So *kerygma* and history are two functions inseparable from the account: the kerygmatic has to be understood as a function and not as the formal notion of the Gospels, since these fall more easily within the notion of theological account than of kerygma.[4]

III. Semantic categories of the New Testament narrative identity

New Testament Christian identity finds its major hermeneutic mode in the account. The 'narrative method' seeks to interpret the biblical narratives today with the help of old and new literary theory; that is, it is concerned with the text as a literary text that can be analysed in literary categories (plot, characters, point of view). Nevertheless, the narrative theological model proper to the New Testament as a whole recounts the subject of Jesus and the origins of the Christian church in the key of fulfilment of the scriptures. This means that each of the literary categories mentioned functions in the narrative as semantic categories, since they are what gives theological meaning to the account. So, bearing in mind that the New Testament is written in a tradition (Old Testament) rather than in a literary form, we need to relate each of these categories to the Old Testament, since each refers understanding of the fact of Christ and the church to a model in the Old Testament tradition. This is what we generally understand by the term 'typology' and the hermeneutic aspect to which it is associated, which sees in persons, facts, happenings and places the prototype, model or figure of historical persons, facts, happenings and places that follow in time. These are related to Christian exegesis of the Old Testament in the New Testament, as they are to classical Christian exegesis.

So the plot or sequential argument of a Gospel is an 'account of happenings', but interpreted narratively as 'fulfilment' in the light of the promise of salvation made by God to the fathers in the old alliance (cf. Luke 1.1; Mark 1.1; Matt. 1.1). The characters, as subjects of the account, act as their characters through typological recourse to the Old Testament. The theological, christological or ecclesiological point of view particular to each of the Gospels is worked out through narrative elaboration of the sources in the light of new recourse to the Old Testament tradition. The facts must equally be distinguished from the typological interpretation given them in the account. The physical setting, whether in time, space or society, can also be a reference to the Old Testament, giving a particular theological character to an account.

IV. The narrative identity of the New Testament Christian communities

Nascent Christianity confessed its faith by telling and re-telling the story of Jesus and of the church of the beginnings. The accounts in the canonical Gospels also reveal a process of faith growing in the re-telling, as shown in their narrative developments and explanations.

Just like Israel, the nascent Christianity of the New Testament also needed some time to complete its clarification of its identity. Let us not forget that until their final expulsion from the synagogue, which did not take place before the last quarter of the first century, the Christians lived within Judaism as just another group. Their difference from other groups, though, lay in their faith in Jesus as the awaited Messiah. On the basis of this faith, the Christian community came to see and to narrate itself as the eschatological people of God, the bearer of the fulfilment of the promises.

1. Mark

The evangelist Mark is the first to join together all the isolated pieces concerning Jesus' life in a continuous narrative with the word *euaggelion* (Mark 1.1) as its heading. This kerygmatic expression, typical of the messianic tradition of the 'herald' of good news (Second and Third Isaiah), gives the character of confession or testimony of faith to the complete account of the story of Jesus. (The Christian account here makes a semantic [derashic] appropriation of the Old Testament tradition concerning the eschatological proclamation of the Kingdom of God in history, applying it to the proclamation of Jesus Christ.) This, then, is a message that is narrative in character and in line with the narrative nature of Old Testament faith. Jesus thereby personifies the good news, the narration of which claims to be the living witness to the working presence of the 'kingdom of God' in his life, actions, death and resurrection (see Mark 1.14–15). Hence the nature of the account as narrative christology: 'the good news of Jesus Christ, the Son of God'.

Mark's plot, which shares little of the suspense technique of modern novels, has to do with human reluctance to accept the messianic identity of Jesus, rejecting him to the point of putting him to a shameful death. To this purpose, the narrator chooses the 'messianic secret' as the dramatic mainspring of his account. This is a specific manner of formulating the development of the progressive revelation of Jesus as the Christ. This, in turn, serves as a spur to the community to accept the difficulties of the present time (persecution, insecurity) and not to concentrate solely on the glorious aspect of Christ now raised and exalted. The present situation has to be endured on the basis of faith in a better future.

2. Matthew

Matthew's Gospel has been described as more ecclesiology than christology. In effect, modern exegesis has pointed out that Matthew has reflected deeply on the consequences the rejection of the Messiah had for Israel and, in parallel with this, has devoted his new account to working out the 'ecclesiological' identity of the Christian community. The narrator has proceeded to transpose the prerogatives of the old Israel, through which it was recognized in the Old Testament tradition as the chosen people, bearer of the people and the kingdom, to the Christian community. The community has to face up to a hostile Judaism which, rejecting Jesus' messiahship, would deny it the status of *ekklesia*. In the final analysis, this is a dispute over the legitimate inheritance of the Old Testament tradition.

Matthew then lays hand on the Old Testament symbol of the 'kingdom of heaven' as the fundamental concept in his narrative ecclesiological account and uses the 'kingdom' to present the Christian community as the people with whom, in Jesus Christ, God has established the new and definitive alliance.[5] Therefore, the community is the *ekklesia* of Jesus (cf. Matt. 16.18; 18.17) in the full historical salvific (and now eschatological) sense of the term, just as it was used to designate Israel in the Old Testament.

3. Luke

Just as Mark narrated the kerygmatic dimension of the life (deeds and words) of Jesus by telling it as 'good news', so Luke gives a kerygmatic dimension to his account through the 'kingdom of God'. In effect, Mark makes the kingdom the content of his 'evangelical' account; Luke, on the other hand, makes the content of the kerygma of the kingdom of God the Easter christology (Jesus dead and raised) and its universal salvific action in taking the good news to the Gentiles (Luke 4.14–44). This is why Luke's account needs the space of two volumes.

Consciousness of the centrality of Christ's pasch in the Christian creed, together with a church implicated in a fully universal mission, made Luke see the need for a new theological account that would respond to the needs of the Christianity of his time. This led him to make full use of the concept of 'the kingdom of God', bringing it up to date by applying it to the current situation. By making christology and ecclesiology the central elements of the kingdom, Luke rendered an inestimable service to the church of his time and of all times by initiating the change from a concept of *basileia* exclusively linked to the *eschaton* (with an exclusively temporal component) to an eminently historical-salvific concept, unfolding dynamically from the presence of Christ to the time of the universal restoration established by God (Acts 3.18–21; Luke 21.29–31).[6]

V. Conclusion

Today, by 'personal identity' we mean 'being myself'. However, the experience each one has of this is different and often remains on a superficial level. In reality, 'being oneself' has to do with the experience of 'making a success of oneself' to which we all aspire, consciously or unconsciously. Now it is possible to distinguish various levels in this quest for personal identity and success: the psychological, the existential, the religious. Here we are concerned with the religious, while bearing in mind that this supposes the other two.

The religious or spiritual dimension of personal identity refers to having understood and accepted that 'I am I beyond myself'. In the final analysis, it is God who enables me to be myself. God is the very source of my freedom. This supposes that I can sustain myself in God, because God is not only not against my freedom (the project of being ourselves authentically) but supports it and is committed to it.

If we accept all this, how do we form the religious identity of modern people today? Scripture has shown us a sort of school for the formation of spiritual identity, since faith forms an essential part of people in the Bible. So reflection on the narrative nature of biblical faith can contribute today to the search for such an identity.

Foundational experiences of God working in their own lives enable believers to narrate/identify themselves in terms of salvation. So believers go on re-telling over and over again their story according to their faith process, since it is natural for religious identity to be expressed in narrative form. This means that 'there is no religion from abstract thought, only from the concrete experience of life, love, and death. God has to be sought.'[7]

Finally, as opposed to those who limit themselves to telling happenings, anecdotes, experiences, because they have no history, believers identified with their faith read their histories in unity of meaning. This is what allows them to discover their lives as a whole as a faith project in search of authentic personal achievement.

Translated by Paul Burns

Notes

1. Pontifical Biblical Commission, *The Interpretation of the Bible in the Church* (1993), 'Conclusion'.
2. Cf. A. de Pury (ed.), *Le Pentateuque en question. Les origines de la composition des cinq livres de la Bible à la lumière des recherches récentes*, Geneva 1989, passim.
3. A. del Agua, *El método midrásico y la exégesis del Nuevo Testamento*, Valencia 1985, passim.
4. E.g., 'narrative christology' in Luke and 'ecclesiology as narrative discourse' in Matthew 13. Cf. del Agua, 'La interpretación del relato en la doble obra lucana', *EstEcl.* 71, 1996, 169–214; 'Eclesiología como discourso narrado: Mt 13.2–52', ibid. 72. 1997, 217–69.
5. Cf. 'God with us': Matt. 1.23; Isa. 8.10; cf. Matt. 28.20.
6. A. del Agua, 'El cumplimiento del Reino de Dios en la misión de Jesús: Programa del evangelio de Lucas (Lc 4.14–44)', *EstBib.* 38, 1979–80, 209–93.
7. J Garrido, *Proceso humano y Gracia de Dios. Apuntes de espiritualidad cristiana*, Santander 1996, 27.

The History of Jesus as the Foundation and Origin of Religious Identity

HERMANN HÄRING

I. Four questions, four answers?

'Then he said to him, "But you, who do you say that I am?" Simon Peter answered, "You are the Messiah, the son of the living God"' (Matt. 16.15f.). This question has been understood in different ways and therefore has been given different answers in the history of Christianity. As an introduction to the discussion I want to refer here to four possibilities.

1. First, the question is apparently simple and elementary: '*Who is Jesus?*' What is his nature? How can and must he be understood, described and therefore preached and believed in? This 'is' question presupposes that the question of the identity of Jesus can be answered clearly in the here and now. Therefore for fifteen hundred years the tradition of the Christian churches has given and still gives an apparently clear, though complex, answer: Jesus is Lord and Messiah (Christ), God's Son and Word, truly God and truly man at the same time. The great Christian tradition which began with the Old Testament and still has not come to a standstill laboured over these answers.

2. Since the eighteenth century, however, a second question with a historical orientation has emerged in the church of the West; for Jesus' question to Peter was put at that time, at the time of Jesus, and primarily has validity for that time. So we have to ask '*Who was Jesus?* What did he do and say, and what happened to him?' The very question has caused considerable unrest. This 'was' question in fact presupposes that the question of Jesus with its biblical orientation must first go by way of a historical account. That caused difficulties. People not only noted what Lessing called the 'deep gulf' between historical and dogmatic faith but also pointed out critically that Jesus' identity cannot always be spoken of in the same way. The Gospels themselves, and even more the New Testament, offer different answers, and biblical answers are hardly comparable with later metaphysical, personalist,

mystical thought or liberation theology. Haven't the answers changed of their own accord? Mustn't the later dogmatic statements be massively corrected by what we know from the earliest testimonies to Jesus? This opposition between the 'Jesus of history' and the 'Christ of dogma' has not been overcome down to the present day.

3. Since historical research into Jesus became established in the nineteenth century, the question has become even more complex. Even Peter gave only one of a number of possible answers, and probably question and answer were only formulated in retrospect, i.e. projected back on the earthly life of Jesus. It has become increasingly clear that we can neither define the identity of Jesus in time nor objectify it. Rather, we are dependent on testimonies and reports and their intentions and situations (the *Sitz im Leben*). So the question increasingly became '*What can we know of Jesus at all* and with what certainty can we appeal to him?' This 'can' question presupposes that our answers in principle remain dependent on limited, contingent historical sources.[1]

4. Finally, the past decades have confronted us with what for the moment is a last experience. We have discovered that Jesus asked his question as a Jew (strictly speaking a 'Jewish Christian') and Peter answered it as a Jew (strictly speaking a 'Jewish Christian'). There is the plurality and contextual conditioning of theological and believing discourse. For a long time we have known that there were and are many different pictures of Jesus alongside the one faith in Jesus Christ regulated by dogma. They are dependent on the times and life-styles, the faith and world-view, of theological, philosophical or aesthetic media in which they have been set down.[2] Theology long understood them as signs of the inner wealth of faith in Christ, as an illustration of the fertility of dogma. Only later did the awareness grow that in different continents, cultures, societies and world-views there *must* be different pictures of Christ which we cannot reduce to one another. I see three reasons for this. Only in this way can we do justice to the diversity and fullness of human existence, which is lived out in a great variety of contexts. Only in this way can we overcome the cultural and ideological limitation of the individual pictures of Jesus. Only in this way can we formulate anew questions and answers about Jesus for a non-Christian and inter-religious public.[3] Now the central question which guides all other questions is: '*How must we and can we speak of Jesus today in the face of different situations?*' However, the question presupposes that we can speak of Jesus' identity only in relation to our own. I shall come back to that later.

So in reflection on the person and cause of Jesus and in the attempt to

define his identity, the history of theology has developed four questions. In
so doing has it also given four disparate answers and thus destroyed the unity
of our faith in Jesus? There is dispute over the answer to this question. It
has to be conceded that critical processes were always at work in the epoch-
making transitions. Of course the christology of the early church (1) already
opposed conflicting conceptions and therefore led to splits which have
lasted to the present day. Of course historical-critical exegesis has embarked
on inexorable criticism of a narrow dogmatic faith in Christ: Jesus of
Nazareth did not have a divine nature (in a metaphysical sense); he is not
God come down from heaven but God's son (in the Jewish sense), fully and
wholly human. Many people today still see the church's belief in Christ
threatened by this. Of course the particular memories of Jesus Christ which
have been handed down have been reduced to a limited number. It is no
longer possible to depict the personality of Jesus or to write a psychology or
even a biography of him (3); we simply know too little about many details –
say about his birth, descent and original social relationships, about his
connections with John the Baptist or the Essenes, about his relationship to
women, about the precise reason for his condemnation – to make precise
statements. Of course over recent decades the impression has arisen that the
identity of Jesus depends on the concrete conditions of our contexts (4); is it
still possible to make any objective statements about the nature of Jesus at
all?

But these transitions have kept deepening the question of Jesus. In its
cultural context the early church was with good reason convinced that
its new christology with an ontological foundation 'breathes scripture'
(Athanasius). Historical exegesis has not led to a loss but to a renewal of
Christian faith. Only now can we reassess the concrete significance of the
fact that God's truth and love become reality in a human being. The more
critically individual texts are investigated and their tendency is perhaps
identified, the more sharply the profile and significance of Jeus of Nazareth
for Christian faith has emerged. For it can now be demonstrated more
clearly than ever how Jesus differs from other founders of religion. And the
more we have become aware of the ideological and cultural conditions of
our talk of Christ, the richer has become the span of what we can call the
identity of Jesus. From a global perspective, at no time since the period of
the New Testament has there been such varied, creative and concrete talk of
Jesus as there is in our day.[4]

These reflections therefore lead to a paradoxical result. Criticism and
humanization, historical-critical concern and respect for the various cul-

tures seem – according to some anxious critics – to destroy the mystery of Jesus, but they have brought about the opposite. Instead of evacuating the answers, they have transformed them in a grandiose way. Today more than ever, theology and the church are capable of taking up even the great impulses of literature, music and the graphic arts. The identity of Jesus has again become richer, the less we fixate the identity of Jesus on metaphysical descriptions of essence, on objective historical information, on comprehensive information or timeless definitions. How is this paradox to be explained? The answer I want to develop here is that the identity of Jesus shows itself not in information or historical precision, but in a threefold process: in a narrative account, in correlation with present-day experience and in connection with each present and new identification. In this threefold way Christians can form an authentic religious identity.

II. From information to narrative

In the theory of language and theology over past decades there has been an intensive investigation of the elementary form of narrative language. The most important results are generally known. First of all the basic situation of all language applies to narrative: there is the triangular situation of 'reference' (the real or supposed reality), 'senders' (who speak or write) and 'recipients' (who hear or listen). At least in the ideal case the senders enter their texts;[5] through these the new audience (hearers or readers) is confronted with the matter or entangled in it. Various things are communicated to them – implicitly or openly, clearly or in complicated mixtures: one might think of information, the expression of feelings or imperatives which are to direct action. Now narratives cannot be reduced either to information, expression or imperatives, for first of all they repeat what has happened (really or in fiction) in the form of language. Thus language takes on laws and form from events. No theory is constructed, no abstraction is analysed, but history is made present. The 'plot' of the course of events, agents and the setting of an event re-emerge. Of course in narrative too there are abstractions or simplified interpretations, and reality is bracketed off. Some reports are too simple to be true. But the common factor in all narratives is that they bring different things together: beginning and end, action and suffering, persons and things, space and time – at any rate when they are together. Presumably the ever-effective factor of time ensures that narratives entangle their hearers (or readers) in what happens in them, in a quite elementary way. Anyone who really wants to understand and follow a story has no choice but to keep thinking from the beginning to the end, to let it arise again at a new point of time so that it takes place again here and now, so that the overall situation is recreated, and they and others identify with the persons in the narrative and understand the whole story as their 'own'. Both tradition and present-day hermeneutics calls this process of appropriation mimesis. According to the above-mentioned triangular situation of original event, narrator (or text) and recipient, three stages are also in play in it.[6]

What have these remarks to do with the identity of Jesus and the identity of Christians? The connection lies in the discovery that we find the identity of Jesus primarily in narrative contexts. I shall not be going here into the structures which Agua describes thoroughly in his article. It clearly emerges from them that the New Testament texts cannot understand the identity of Jesus without retelling the Jewish tradition.[7] I am interested in something else: the person, cause and fate of Jesus are not presupposed as known in the Gospels, nor is there a timeless argument in them. Nor do Jesus' person, cause and fate appear as past history. The very way in which these are interlocked with Jewish tradition (at that time still fully present and effective, alive) shows that the person and cause of Jesus *are* the story in which the audience – if they want to understand it – are completely and unconditionally entangled. So anyone who wants to know who Jesus is, is told that he spoke of God's salvation and dealt with people who unawares became the audience he addressed. He has meals with them, he heals the sick and turns to the needy; he awakens joyful hope. He goes through the country with a group of people who have no possessions and sometimes separates from them to pray. He warns, perhaps threatens and forgives sins in the name of God. With other members of his people he endures conflicts and as a pious Jew also goes on pilgrimage to Jerusalem. Finally, to the great horror of his followers, he is killed, and they experience him as the Risen One to whom God gives his due. Certainly all these individual stories, like the accounts as a whole, are carefully composed and thought through; scholars have discovered distinctive pictures of Jesus in each Gospel and in individual source texts. Everywhere there are interpretations which are theological, strictly Jewish, critical of the Jews, social or political. But nowhere is the narrative form abandoned. The narratives remain the decisive medium; they neither become a goal or an illustration but remain the sphere in which constantly new, indefinable identifications can take place: with those who follow him.[8]

An age in which scientifically assured insights play a central role thus has problems, for stories never lead to any definitive information. Rather, they open up possibilities of interpretation and different reactions. The question of the identity of Jesus remains open: it is an identity which shows itself in action and conduct.[9] It is left to individual readers or a reading community to decide where Jesus is 'divine', where he is a 'model' or a warning, where he goes with me or against me. We cannot say or establish definitively or objectively who Jesus is. At any rate, in connection with the great Jesus narrative itself, there is a process of ever-closer focus. The death of Jesus is the moment of the greatest clarity, but precisely at that point he falls silent and knows (according to Mark) that he is abandoned by God; even now it is left to readers to form their own judgment. The course of Jesus' life runs contrary to all human criteria. But why have the readers first of all (and in the individual narratives) been left to the criteria of an utterly human history?

We shall not investigate these questions further but keep to just one conclusion. If the thesis of the elementary significance of the Jesus narrative holds, and if narratives lead to ever new and open identifications, then the later highly speculative christology was perhaps not wrong (questions of heresy or orthodoxy are not in place), but it failed to recognize the elementary significance of the narrative sources. The paradox that criticism of christological information has not dissolved the memory of Jesus but deepened it is thus understandable. The goal of a good theology can only be to protect from misuse or contempt the narrative of Jesus as the report of human salvation. Unfortunately in modern times classical christology has increasingly taken the place of the Jesus stories and thus suppressed them. The investigation of the Jesus of history was therefore necessary and overdue.

III. From narrative to experience

The identity of Jesus is a narrated and thus an open identity. How are we to understand that in concrete terms? The openness of all narratives has long been felt in theology to be a disturbing problem. Now it is one of the fundamental insights of modern hermeneutics that – to put it in an abstract way – understanding does not lead to repetition but to ever-new interpretation. New interpretation always means conversation, appropriation and therefore a constant process of new beginning and criticism. Already two generations ago Bultmann emphatically made it clear that processes of understanding are always provisional. As he said, they keep leading to a new self-understanding which cannot be objectified; nor can their content be exhausted. Understanding may not be trivialized so that it becomes a harmless getting to know; it remains rooted in attempts and fragments, paradoxes and contradictions. In this way he anticipated postmodern positions.[10] This warning was not taken seriously, but in a conservative hermeneutics gave the impression that in understanding we come ever closer to a matter. So it was thought that good exegesis could investigate the confession of Jesus Christ ever more precisely, and that finally we must achieve the goal of the one true christology.[11] That had earlier proved to be a deception, and it is only the consistent christology from below which has shattered this deceptive hope.[12] Schillebeeckx gave classical formulation to the reason: strictly speaking the Gospels do not report what Jesus did, said or suffered. However, the reason for that does not lie in the limitations of the witnesses, in their prejudice or ideological blindness, but in the fact that reports always offer more than pure facts; what they offer is different. The reports in the Gospels tell us the *experience* of Jesus had through the narrators themselves who followed him.[13] Here Schillebeeckx provided a key word without which the depth structure of a narrative, even that of the Jesus narratives, cannot be grasped.

Narratives disclose themselves in ever-new experiences, thus in ever-new perspectives which are given to us by our physical, cultural or temporal situation. A simple event – the football in the goal – can mean a victory for some and a defeat for others. In a legal judgment justification and condemnation stand over against each other in perspective. The birth of a child may mean joy for the father and pain or death for the mother. What is new in a narrative, the elements of discontinuity and creativity, grows out of the process of appropriation in which people mould one perspective into another; indeed they have to do this if the narrative is not to fall silent. For these perspectives are either physically, culturally or temporally conditioned; in other words they are either Semitic or Hellenistic, mediaeval or modern European or South Indian, male or female, shaped by success or by misery. Even Jesus' death can be unfolded from the experience of subjection or liberation, abandonment or self-surrender.

So we shall always experience the identity of Jesus anew and in a different way; there is also a biographical growth of fiath.[14] The Christian message is never there as a pure nucleus, just as even in a prism there is not the refraction of light as such.[15] Thus the overwhelming diversity of pictures of Jesus, i.e. of 'identities' of Jesus, is quite understandable and legitimate. The problem of past pictures of Jesus in Christian piety often lies in the fact that they have been dismissed as irrational, forced to the periphery of faith and church and measured by complicated theoretical constructions. In the meantime we have learned to deal positively with the diversity of such pictures, and thus with the diversity of Christian identity.

The conclusions for the question who we think Jesus to be are far-reaching and must not be underestimated. Today we must begin with the fourth of the questions posed at the beginning. The identity of Jesus is rightly formed anew in every age and every culture – depending on its individual, collective, social, cultural or sexual character. Here Jesus in principle is given as many answers to the question of his identity as people who identify with him. But these uncounted 'identities' fit into the network of classical, comprehensive or far-reaching pictures of identity which have formed or re-formed in the course of time. These symbols assume a representative function. They function as summaries of elements and reminiscences, of values and expectations, which put the narratives of Jesus' action and words in wider religious, moral and individual contexts. Jesus then becomes the 'messiah' or 'king', 'brother' or friend', the bearer of the Spirit or the one who makes God's truth present, the one who is despised and tortured. This symbolic world in which the identity of Jesus is constantly summed up anew stands as it were midway between the basic reports and a reflective theology.[16] These symbols are not static concepts or pictures with 'surplus value'. They are linguistic or semiotic events which collect what is narrated and at the same time identify experiences. Their power lies in this twofold function, one narrative and one appropriative or mimetic. Symbols direct inner discoveries outwards, and thus make it possible to grasp, discuss, communicate them. Peter says, 'You are the anointed, the son of God!' In so doing he pours his (i.e. early Christian) experiences into a sign which takes up countless earlier memories. Therefore such a symbolism – standing between memory and theology – has the character of a response, not that of narrative or reflection. All symbols respond to the situation that they identify. That brings us to the last point, in which what has been said so far is given its unity.

IV. Identification as a process of relationship

The classical doctrine of Jesus came to grief – at any rate in modern times – on its inappropriate questioning. It focussed on reflection instead of on symbolic collection. It wanted to work out independent information instead of relying on narrative. It gave the impression that the identity of Jesus was an objective datum. Here already the question of God should have made us more cautious. For independently of hermeneutical considerations one thing has not been disputed: God cannot be objectified, because God transcends all understanding. How could it be possible to objectify the one who according to the classical tradition has been identified wholly in terms of God? But as soon as we take seriously the narrative character of the message of Jesus and understand the christological symbolism as a human answer, another connection appears. As we have seen in many articles in this issue, no human person stands simply in or of himself or herself. We identify ourselves through our actions, through our relationships, through the symbol-systems that surround us, through our social situation and through the way in which others identify us. In addition there is an aspect which is topical for Western cultures. The weaker the cultural and collective symbols become, and the more our societies lose their institutionally static focal points, the more we are thrown back on ourselves in identifying ourselves and others. Thus what remains for us is not a reflection on our personhood (the concept has lost all viable contours) nor reflection on our social position, but reflection on our own action, our validity for others, on the destiny of our life. What follows from that for the way of Christian faith?

In contrast to other world religions Christianity knows a single person as the criterion and source of its religious identity. Granted, Christian faith too, like other religions, is a way of life, a comprehensive orientation on reality which can be identified and a 'way' related to an ultimate authority in which the world is sustained. But only in Christianity are these dimensions (including faith in God) held together in a historical-personal relationship. A Christian is someone who identifies himself or herself with Jesus Christ by being identified by Jesus Christ. This conception can be convincing only on two presuppositions: on the one hand – as I have already said – we understand the identity of a person not as a static, even ontological, datum, but as the result of a relationship which is experienced and expressed symbolically. I become myself by finding myself in my relations to other people and can name these. On the other hand, also as I have already said, the identity of Jesus is not closed, but keeps arising anew for believers in the interplay of memory and symbolization. In this way no unwanted identity is painted over the Jesus of Christian faith; nor is his identity handed over to the mere whim of present-day Christians. This relationship does not arise as feeling or as a heroic act of will. It arises by really taking the history of Jesus seriously through experiencing righteousness in a new life. What I mean is 'discipleship', i.e. a way of life which – we hope – succeeds in making this identification in an existential experiment. Only in this way, in the new person, does he become 'way', 'truth' and 'life'.

However, at this point a new discussion of the question should really begin, about how such identification takes place in practice. Already in the framework of his discussion of the symbolization of evil, Paul Ricoeur pointed out that we human beings – as beings with bodies and located in a particular place – can come to ourselves as it were only 'indirectly'. A direct, unmediated and absolutely transparent inner relationship to our self is impossible. The same goes for the process of identification. I can never arrive at myself by fixing myself directly and immediately on myself. Anyone who wants to identify with Jesus in pure inwardness will depersonalize him and end up in empty moralism, fundamentalism or escapism. Those who attempt the identification or want it to happen to them and above all anyone who – in our era – expects it on new presuppositions and in a new way cannot do this without an openness that takes all possibilities into account. I call this openness the power of imagination. What I mean is not a fantasy which arises from our immediate needs, but the imagination which enters into the world, explores its boundaries and discovers new possibilities in the unexpected and unaccustomed.[17]

Presumably the capacity and the fertility of the imagination go together with the deepest experience, analysed by Paul Ricoeur, that we remain ourselves only if and when we constantly change. Identification as the gift of finding ourselves therefore presupposes the imagination of new possibilities, which are not imprisoned in the nightmare of the past, but in which Ernst Bloch discovers the field of the coming and the unexpected..[18] There is no Christianity viable for the future without imagination.

So let us take seriously the medium of narrative reminiscence, as the Gospels, as the basis of Christian faith. It again follows from this that in Christian faith our and Jesus' identity are related. If it is already true in the human sphere generally that being a person implies interpersonality, that is even more true in Christian faith.[19] Therefore they are not independent of each other but go together and can only be discussed together. For this reason Jesus was once called the 'man for others' and there was talk of his 'pro-existence'. That is first of all a very human definition, for we are all 'men for others', and none of us (not even Jesus) can appeal to an identity which is sufficient in itself. Therefore, rightly understood, the scheme of the Christian life is built on a deeply human foundation. Only by following it can a moral or a specifically religious identification be successful. Religious quality has such an identity when in it limit experiences find their place, their assimilation and their home: I am thinking of experiences of life and death, of limitation and going beyond limits, of being given and being taken, of hopeless injustice and final desperation. It is the discovery that even in these destructive, indeed annihilating, limit experiences we remain ourselves and come to ourselves. We can speak of explicitly religious identity when the question of God becomes the explicit theme in this context. Since Jesus, as has been said, can be symbolized as the 'man for others', religious and 'purely human' identity in fact come to coincide with him. Christians therefore do well to take seriously the 'purely human' impulses in our cultures as a source of religious experience of the world and therefore also to accept other religions as the way of salvation.

Conclusion

We have come to the conclusion that Jesus' identity can be discussed and seen where men and women identify with him or by him, i.e. where they find themselves again with their hopes and expectations, in his memory. This is not yet intrinsically a religious process: Christian faith can take place in a deeply human process of mutual identification which can also occur between lovers or friends, travelling companions or sufferers. Doesn't that say too little? Doesn't the significance of Jesus of Nazareth lie in the fact that in him something deeply godly, i.e. the ultimate mystery, becomes evident with a directness which not is attained elsewhere? Yes, that is correct, but this mystery, too, does not show itself in an objective way which is at our disposal or impossible to misunderstand. Therefore it is worth the trouble of looking in the Gospels also for those sources in which Jesus does not relate to other men and women, does not speak with them or argue with them. We must also seek those sources in which the report of Jesus gives up something of his own mystery – let us call it the divine.

Here two sources are important for me. One is that famous passage in which Jesus thanks his 'Abba' for having granted this only to the little ones (Matt. 11.25–27). These verses in fact indicate an inner relationship to God in which others so to speak have to seek no more: 'All things have been given me by my Father . . .' According to Schillebeeckx, Jesus shifts the epicentre of his life to God.[20] At this point a foretaste of Jesus' faith comes to bear. In the light of that we can identify ourselves by Jesus but not vice versa. In him we can come to ourselves.

The other source is made up of the parables. They are about the kingdom of heaven and the joy of the meal, about running away and coming back, about losing and finding, about guilt and forgiveness. Something quite striking takes place in them. Jesus speaks of himself by telling stories about acting and being together, about dealings with others. Precisely by speaking in such an utterly worldly way, i.e. incorporating everyday events into his imagination, he speaks of 'God'. So he does not say who God is as an informant giving definitions. Rather, he entangles us as a narrator in the question of how we can interpret God's action. Thus in Jesus we experience a start on those who develop their own identity in and by him. It is a start which we do not find in our human or religious identity (i.e. that which is related to God). Therefore Jesus of Nazareth, according to Christian conviction, speaks clearly, as it were officially, in the name of God. However, anyone can also have this start over fellow human beings, for 'what you have done to the least of these my brothers and sisters your have done to me' (Matt. 25.40). Thus religious identity begins where 'normal' human identity discovers an unfathomable depth in itself and expresses it. Perhaps that is why the story of Jesus has become the story of a new religious identity, because it filled out the possibilities of human imagination in an unexpected way without dissolving them in it. God is a Deus *humanissimus*.[21] Perhaps for that reason Jesus has become the symbol of the truly divine which at the same time is truly human, what we all hope for equally and without rivalry.

Translated by John Bowden

Notes

1. For the overall situation see W. Jeanrond and C. Theobald (eds), *Who Do You Say That I Am?*, *Concilium* 1997/1.
2. Hans Küng, *On Being a Christian*, London and New York 1977, 117–44; J. Pelikan, *Jesus through the Centuries*, New Haven and London 1985; for Jesus in literature see K.-J. Kuschel, *Jesus im Spiegel der Weltliteratur*, Düsseldorf 1999.
3. The new quality of the 'third' quest of Jesus appears in its 'postmodernist' integration of a great variety of theological approaches from past decades. It not only makes comprehensive use of classical historical sources (Bible, apocrypha, Judaica, archaeology), but also uses the approaches of sociological criticism, history of religions, liberation theology, feminism and interfaith studies. Whether the historical paradigm of objective research into Jesus is completely outdated in my view still needs extensive discussion. For an introduction and bibliography see S. Freyne, 'The Quest of the Historical Jesus. Some Theological Reflections', *Concilium* 1997/1 (n.1), 37–51.
4. A look at the Internet at the first attempt showed me 950 books on the question of Jesus in print. The quality of these books may vary widely. The interest in writing and reading about him is beyond dispute in countries whose culture, constitution and understanding of society is generally said to be secularized.

5. For an introduction to theological hermeneutics and language see I. U. Dalferth, *Religiöse Rede von Gott*, Munich 1981.

6. H. Haker works out this connection in her article on narrative and moral identity in Paul Ricoeur, above, 59–68.

7. If I understand the article by A. del Agua in this issue rightly, this does not degrade the Old Testament to the past but empowers it for a present which is still indispensable. Therefore it would be better to speak of the 'Old' Testament rather than of the Jewish Bible.

8. This mode of identification is preferred by the New Testament model of discipleship and corresponds to the later situation of a church which is gradually developing into a distinguishable social form. The model of discipleship needs to be protected against the misunderstanding of the heroic bringer of salvation and acts as an antidote to sacralized theories of redemption which have been analysed in a masterly way by René Girard. This does not exclude other modes of identification. For example, at a very early stage Francis was understood as 'another Christ'. Suffering men and women and those fighting in solidarity could never be prevented from identifying themselves with Jesus.

9. So formally this is not an identity which can be fixed legally, psychologically or sociologically, nor an identity of subject in the philosophical sense of the word.

10. P. Chatelion Counet, *De sarcofaag van het Woord. Postmoderniteit, desconstructie en het Johannesevangelie*, Kampen 1995, 252–90.

11. This concern comes out well in the 'theologies' of the Old and New Testament and in the New Testament christologies. For them, too, as Albert Schweitzer already discovered in the quest of the historical Jesus, in fact, despite every desire for objectivity, each of these schemes develops only its preformed concept.

12. In my view this problem is discussed in a classical, though also concealed, way in Hans Küng's arguments about christology, see H. Haring, *Hans Küng. Breaking Through*, London 1998, 142–8.

13. E. Schillebeeckx, *Jesus*, London 1979, 43–61.

14. J. Fowler, *Stages of Faith*, New York and London 1981, has gained classic importance as a study of the psychology of religion. This analysis can also be applied to Christian faith which – on the basis of this development – identifies with the memory of Jesus.

15. E. Schillebeeckx, *Theologisch geloofsverstaan anno 1983*, Nijmegen 1983.

16. H. Häring, 'Tussen identiteit en verbeelding. Waartoe dient de christologie?', *Tijdschrift voor Theologie* 30, 1999, 358–80.

17. Iris Murdoch in her philosophical work refers to this difficulty.

18. E. Bloch, *The Principle of Hope*, Oxford 1985, Chapter 14.

19. Schillebeeckx, *Jesus* (n.15), 650.

20. Ibid., 658.

21. Ibid., 671.

Identity in Feminist Theological Debate[1]

CHRISTINE FIRER-HINZE

Feminism contributes to Christian understandings of human identity by probing the implications of gender and sexuality for the construal of personhood, and for social systems in which identities are shaped and expressed. Contemporary feminist liberationist[1] theologians affirm theological anthropology's traditional work of delineating features of humanity shared by all.[2] But these scholars bring to the fore the impact of sex/gender on interpretations of humanity, in terms of three complex realities that frame the terrains in which identity is forged and understood: difference, marginality and dynamics of power. In the face of these three realities, feminist theologians insist that adequate Christian articulations of sex/gender and identity can emerge only in communities practising reflective, incarnational solidarity. Theoretical articulations of the human must unfold in contact with, and accountability to, the concrete lives and daily struggles of women and men, what Ada Maria Isasi-Diaz calls the *lo cotidiano y la lucha*, from and for which the most trustworthy theologizing takes place.[3]

Feminist theological debate uncovers four crucial points concerning treatments of human identity in relation to sex/gender:

1. Apprehensions of human identity in relation to sex/gender must be framed by struggles for right understanding and practice concerning difference.

Contemporary theologians treat sex/gender neither reductively nor univocally. Many otherwise widely varying Catholic discussions of sex/gender do assume that sex/gender has an impact on identity, and many affirm the existence of certain fundamental differences between male and female human beings. This being so, gender-focussed theological analyses of identity must not only explore asymmetries in men's and women's ascribed qualities, behaviour, roles, or status. Such analysis must also ask which asymmetries, if any, spring from authentic differences, and/or generalized and unchangeable characteristics of men and women, and are therefore legitimate; which rest on actual differences that are manipulated and exploited for the benefit of some and the oppression of others, and are thus illegitimate; and which reflect differences that are culturally constructed and reproduced, and therefore subject to ongoing re-examination and revision.

Feminist theologians regard difference itself as a necessary and rich resource. Elizabeth Johnson invokes Audre Lorde's wisdom on this point:

> Difference must be not merely tolerated, but seen as a fund of necessary polarities between which our creativity can spark like a dialectic. . . . Only within that interdependency of different strengths, acknowledged and equal, can the power to seek new ways of being in the world be generated. . . . Difference is that raw and powerful connection from which our personal power is forged.[4]

M. Shawn Copeland concurs, arguing that 'difference is the authentic context for interdependence'; indeed, 'the interdependence of difference is a crucial condition for realizing our very full humanity'.[5] For feminist theologians, the plurality of identity consists in more than sexual or gender difference, but certainly includes these. And, as in the human sciences, one discovers a range of theological positions on the significance of sexual difference for personal identities and social roles.

Liberal feminists, underscoring human commonality, regard sex/gender as accidental to human identity, and without necessary import for social roles.[6] A second feminist position regards cultural interpretations of bodily-rooted sex distinctions as propagating gendered differences in experience, thought, and practice by positioning women as the primary bearers of certain human values and characteristics, such as nurturing and caring practices, culturally designated as 'feminine'.[7] In a third construction, Pope John Paul II and like-minded Catholic theologians posit an ontological significance to sex/gender, that fits men and women for complementary but different religiously-symbolic mediations, forms of authority, and familial or societal roles. The pope affirms that 'womanhood and manhood are complementary not only from the physical and psychological points of view, but also from the ontological . . .' This complementarity is 'iconic', warranting a 'certain diversity of roles [which] is in no way prejudicial to women, provided that this diversity is not the result of an arbitrary imposition, but is rather an expression of what is specific to being male or female'.[8] Theologians who elaborate this position perceive in sexed/gendered identity a primordial symbolic truth about the nuptial relationality of humanity itself, reflective of the covenantal-nuptial relation between God and humanity, and Christ and the church.[9] Being male or female has profound religious significance which, if ignored or contravened (for instance, by women's participation in the sacramental priesthood), tragically distorts both Christian and human community.

Feminist theologians affirm the impact of sex/gender difference on identity, but reject rigid metaphysical, religious or social determinations of sex/gender's meanings. These scholars propose that men's and women's identities are grounded in but not determined by the specificity of their distinct sexed bodies. Striving to transcend both unipolar and binary understandings of sex and gender, Johnson, for instance, describes a multipolar anthropology of which sexual and gender characteristics are one of a number of dynamic basic features. She proffers a picture of 'one human nature celebrated in an interdependence of multiple differences'; 'not a binary view of two forever predetermined male and female natures, nor abbreviation to a single ideal, but a diversity of ways of being human'. All persons are constituted by a number of mutually-conditioning anthropological constants that include bodiliness and hence sex and race. In Johnson's model, 'sexuality is integrated into a wholistic vision of human persons instead of being made the touchstone of personal identity and thus distorted'.[10] Since the fluidity of gender identity is both constrained and enabled by the sexed body, Miroslav Volf agrees that 'we must both assert that the differences between men and women are irreducible, and refuse to spell out in advance what these differences are'.[11]

2. Articulations of human identity in relation to sex/gender must be framed by struggles for right understanding and practice concerning marginalization and margins.

Marginalization signals forced and destructive exclusion of some by others. Yet margins themselves can be privileged positions for seeing and hearing; boundaries that establish identity and healthy connection; frontiers from which critique and efforts at resistance and transformation may be launched, fences with gates (or selectively permeable boundaries) that are salutary sites for enriching one's understanding of what being human is about, and for struggling to live in authentically human ways. In considering the impact of gender/sex distinctions on identity and practice, feminists distinguish margins as differentiation 'which makes for the separating-and-binding that results in patterns of interdependence' and ensures identity and stable

boundaries, from marginalization as exclusion which betrays interdependence by withdrawing from, cutting off, or eliminating the other; or
pseudo-inclusion that transgresses authentic separation by assimilating or
subjugating the otherness of the other.[12] Judgment, honed within a truth-
seeking community, fosters the capacity to discriminate between authentic
and fraudulent inclusion and differentiation, and impels struggle against
destructive practices of marginalization.

*3. Articulations of human identity in relation to sex/gender must emerge
from amid a struggle for right understanding and practice with respect to
dynamics of power.*

The importance of analysing relations and effects of power as these are
inscribed in both affirmative human identity, and in that which crushes and
corrupts identity, cannot be overestimated. Theological anthropologies
not attuned to dynamics of power as it enables and constrains, shapes and
shatters human be-ing in concrete circumstances are at best abstract and
anaemic, at worst imperialist and pernicious. Astute power analysis contributes indispensably to robust understandings of sexed/gendered identity
capable of grounding authentic, justice-seeking discipleship.

*4. Truthfully and justly to apprehend human identity in relation to
sex/gender requires communal practices of reflective solidarity.*

Especially as articulated by liberationist feminist theologians, solidarity
emerges amid responsible, power-attuned engagement in the plurality of
'we's' that identify us. Reflective solidarity entails a further demand: that
dialogical engagements be bordered and challenged by disciplined advertence to what political theorist Jodi Dean calls 'a situated third'.[13] The
situated third represents a place to be given, in thought and practice, to
the presence of others whom any particular 'we' does not encompass. To
exercise reflective solidarity entails active concern for how that marginalized
other might be respected, if not included. Unlike the 'neutral third' or
'generalized other' proposed by Jürgen Habermas or George Herbert Mead,
the situated third – like the dialogical partners forming a particular 'we' – is
contextualized, in particular circumstances, and represents the specific
needs and questions of persons which a given dialogue may not be taking
into account. Inviting and requiring thinking about and acting in relation to
this situated third fruitfully de-stabilizes any given 'we' by reminding its

members of others outside, and pressing them to think and act in ways that those others into account.

For feminists, this means that affirmations of gender or sexual identity must be critically solidaristic internally, among the many groups that compose 'women'. One credibly says 'we women' only amid collaborative practices that expose and combat the exclusionary or homogenizing tendencies in saying 'we', tendencies to which speakers from among socially dominant groups are especially prone.[14] This requires privileged women to cultivate virtues of teachability and earthy humility in relating to their sisters in non-dominant groups. Reflective solidarity further requires that as feminists reconceive human identity, the situated other implied by the 'we' of women – men, in all their concrete differences – be responsibly taken into account. Solidarity thus encompasses a reflective component that construes identity in terms of the 'we's that I share in by reason my sexual orientation, culture, gender, life circumstance, age, religion, etc.; while distinguishing the non-'we's created by my participation in some groups and not in others. It also involves a component of moral responsibility whereby perceiving, judging and acting accountably in relation to those composing a given 'we' occurs with respectful advertence to those not composing it.

Understood as reflection and practice embodying mutual accountability in relationship, solidarity is something that those on the margins, whom dominant cultures brand as different or other, are especially able to appreciate. Marginalized persons are also keenly attuned to instances of sham or failed solidarity and their consequences.[15] In this vein, feminist theologians increasingly look to multi-racial feminism as a locus for leadership and insight concerning practices and relations of solidarity capable of creating the conditions for adequately understanding the 'human' as male and female, gay and straight, in varying class, racial-ethnic, and cultural situations.[16]

Any satisfactory grasp of human identity as sexual or gendered can issue only from such a hermeneutical and practical commitment to what Dean calls 'the fallible, situated, and open-ended conversation of humanity'.[17] Solidarity presses the power-advantaged party in any interchange to resist monological speech and action in favour of the struggle for complex dialogical mutuality. By finding non-oppressive ways to lean over or reach through the fences that separate us, dialogical solidarity uncovers the grounds for new particular solidarities grounded in either affectional or conventional ties.[18] These connections, to be truly responsible, must occur the reflective presence of the situated third, who represents the perspective and concerns of those that this particular 'we' is most in danger of marginalizing. So understood, reflective solidarity enacts the hermeneutical and practical privilege of the poor and oppressed, and the gospel demand for a preferential option for the poor.

Simultaneously, this articulation acknowledges that amidst systemic patterns of domination and constraint, power relations also exist in shifting and criss-crossing micro-patterns which embed the agential identity of each societal member. Reflective, dialogical solidarity illumines the power of seemingly powerless women, including poor women or publicly-obscured workers in the care economy. Young Jamaican women providing home care for affluent but frail white senior citizens in New York City, or Latina women in their activity and authority within the circle of *familia/comunidad*, or indeed women in most families, routinely find themselves in relations of profound power-advantage as so often they literally hold in their hands the lives and psyches of those whom they tend and serve. Wherever macro- or micro-relations place agents in positions of power-advantage, reflective solidarity demands practices of humility, listening, repentance, respectful space-giving, making way, giving and receiving. Wherever one's circumstances reflect power-disadvantage, reflective solidarity demands self-esteem, courage, boldness, speaking the truth, resistance, forgiveness, patience. As women and men engage in dialogue from differently-powered positions, the face and voice of the situated third to that dialogue shifts. And as members of historically powerful and members of historically subjugated groups risk leaning over fences towards one another, seeking to discover tenuous threads of connection, solidarity demands that those connections be continually challenged and stretched through accountable engagement with the situated other.

Reflective solidarity as the matrix for properly envisaging human identity disintegrates if it remains merely in individual heads. As Copeland reminds us, solidarity is a wrenching, ever-threatened task, 'the achievement of community'.[19] Cultivating communities of reflective solidarity requires members willing continually undertake to anew the arduous and messy work of responsibly living between and among the varied solidarities that comprise the 'we's in which the richness of any 'I' appears. Trinh T. Minh-ha describes this dynamic movement among solidarities as an intervention which impacts our very apprehension of identity by undercutting the inside-outside opposition. It creates an 'inappropriate' other or same who moves about with always at least two gestures: that of affirming 'I am like you' while persisting in her difference, and that of reminding others that 'I am different', while unsettling every definition of otherness arrived at.[20]

Solidaristic theory and practice pave the necessary and most promising road towards a reliable and just Christian apprehension of human sexed and gendered identity. This claim is being voiced today by feminists across a range of fields. Most significantly, it is a claim embodied and borne out in the thinking and acting in solidarity that takes place in the daily lives of many, especially women and others in marginalized situations.

Feminists appropriating sex/gender into theological treatments of identity are recognizing that only within reflection and practice in solidarity can humanity as male and female be truthfully glimpsed and responsibly theorized. Conceived from this standpoint, under concrete conditions of finitude, sin and grace, human identity appears simultaneously in its consoling and exhilarating commonality, and its dangerous, beautiful diversity. Embracing such a vision, women and men, by God's grace, are empowered to reflect more luminously the glory of the image and likeness of God.

Notes

1. This article emphasizes North American womanist, *mujerista*, and Euro-American feminist theologians, but 'feminist liberationist' refers to woman-centred, justice-seeking theological approaches erupting across the globe. See Elisabeth Schüssler Fiorenza (ed.), *The Power of Naming: A Concilium Reader in Feminist Liberation Theology*, Maryknoll, NY 1996.

2. Theologically, this affirmation of shared humanity rests on faith in the One whom Katie Geneva Cannon names 'The God Who is Present in the Midst of the Storm', and Linda Moody calls 'The God Who Knows [and is] the Truth'. See Moody, 'Toward a Methodology for Doing Theology Across the Bounds of Difference', in M. A. Hinsdale and P. H. Kaminski (eds.), *Women and Theology*, Annual Publication of the College Theology Society, Vol. 40, 1995, 194, 200 n. 26.

3. See Ada Maria Isasi-Diaz, 'Elements of a *Mujerista* Anthropology', in Ann O'Hara Graff (ed.), *In the Embrace of God: Feminist Approaches to Theological Anthropology*, Maryknoll, NY 1995, 90–102.

4. Audre Lorde, *Sister Outsider*, Freedom, CA 1984, 111–12; cited in Elizabeth Johnson, *She Who Is: The Mystery of God in Feminist Theological Discourse*, New York 1993, 156.

5. M. Shawn Copeland, 'Difference as a Category in Critical Theologies for the Liberation of Women', in Elisabeth Schüssler Fiorenza and M. Shawn Copeland (eds.), *Feminist Theology in Different Contexts*, Concilium 1996/1, 150.

6. See Anne E. Carr, *Transforming Grace: Christian Tradition and Women's Experience*, San Francisco 1990; Susan Moller Okin, *Justice, Gender and the*

Family, New York 1989; Amy R. Baehr, `Toward a New Feminist Liberalism', *Hypatia* 11.1, 1996, 49–66.

7. See esp. Jean Baker Miller, *Toward a New Psychology of Women*, Boston ²1986; cf. Carol Gilligan, *In a Different Voice*, Cambridge, Mass. 1982.

8. Pope John Paul II, *Letter to Women*, Washington, DC 1995, nos.7, 11. Cf. Pope John Paul II, *On the Dignity and Vocation of Women*, Boston 1988.

9. See Monica Migliorino Miller, *Sexuality and Authority in the Catholic Church*, Scranton 1995; Benedict Ashley, OP, *Justice in the Church: Gender and Participation*, Washington, DC 1996.

10. Johnson, *She Who Is* (n.4), 153, 156. Cf. Lisa Sowle Cahill, *Sex, Gender, and Christian Ethics*, New York 1995, ch.4.

11. Miroslav Volf, *Exclusion and Embrace: A Theological Exploration of Identity, Otherness, and Reconciliation*, Nashville 1996, 175, 183.

12. Ibid., 67; 64–71. Cf. Copeland, 'Difference' (n.5), 24–7; Darryl M. Trimiew, *Voices of the Silenced: The Responsible Self in a Marginalized Society*, Cleveland 1993.

13. Jodi Dean, *Solidarity of Strangers: Feminism After Identity Politics*, Berkeley 1996, ch. 1.

14. Iris Marion Young exposes unconscious dynamics of racism, sexism and homophobia in *Justice and the Politics of Difference*, Princeton 1990, ch. 5.

15. Copeland and Dean cite Lynet Uttal, 'Nods That Silence', in Gloria Anzaldua (ed.), *Making Face, Making Soul*, San Francisco, 1990, 317–21, on manipulative ploys at solidarity, especially those directed by white women towards 'red, brown, yellow, and black women'. See Copeland, 'Difference' (n.5), 24–6; Dean, *Solidarity* (n.13), 30–3.

16. See Michael A. Messner, *The Politics of Masculinities: Men in Movements*, Thousand Oaks, CA 1997; Maxine Baca Zinn and Bonnie Thornton Dill, 'Theorizing Difference From Multicultural Feminism,' *Feminist Studies* 22.2, 1992, 321–31.

17. Dean, *Solidarity* (n.13), 143.

18. Ibid., 19–34; cf. Ada Maria Isasi-Diaz, *Mujerista Theology*, Maryknoll, NY 1996, 86–8.

19. Copeland, 'Difference' (n.5), 29–30.

20. Trinh T. Min-ha, 'Not-You/Like You: Post-Colonial Women and the Interlocking Questions of Identity and Difference', in Anzaldua (ed.), *Making Face* (n.15), 375.

Being and Becoming a Self in an Ethical Perspective

HANS G. ULRICH

If human 'identity' is becoming the theme at present, this is both a critical remembrance and a warning. It focusses attention on the insight that in times of unforeseeable change, uprooting and mobilization, in times of a loss of tradition and worlds, in times of any kind of pluralism and in times of an all-embracing competitiveness according to the laws of the market economy, it becomes urgently necessary for people to reflect on identity, without which human life is impossible.[1] The question of identity presupposes that human life is endangered if it loses all form, if it becomes amorphous, if it is a prey to any change, any influence, any intervention. Human life would not be seen realistically if it were denied the need of forms and shapes of identity in which people find themselves and maintain themselves, in terms of which they can be expressed, and in which it becomes evident what they 'are' for themselves and others. If this does not happen, then human beings become anonymous, interchangeable; without such an identity they also become manipulable, as it were shapeless plastic which can be bent into this form or that. This is betrayed by the many kinds of talk about 'shaping' life.

Critical and warning talk of identity raises the question what in these times of a change of tradition, of growing flexibility and anonymity, it means not to be 'something' but someone, or what it means for the communities in which men and women live not just to fulfil some function which is determined from outside but to be a living community which gives individuals part of their identity. In any case, 'being someone' cannot remain a black box, something abstract, something that we perhaps note, as happens in the demand to respect human beings as persons with no indication of what this entails and how it is to be achieved. This personhood and these forms of life are put in danger by being left indefinite desiderata.

The all-important question is how human personhood and human community emerge as being a *self*, how persons and communities are present to others in their selfhood, how they can be heard with their voice and come into view. So this critical remembrance cannot aim at an abstract identity, with human beings perhaps remaining the same; human beings must become a 'self' and keep and live out this self for themselves and others in all necessary changes and learning processes.[2] The same is true of particular communities; however, this does not mean that we should talk of a 'collective' identity – that remains a separate chapter of critical reflection. Nevertheless we need to ask what the self of communities can be. What characterizes the Christian church, what characterizes Christians as community? How far are Christians in their understanding of church and community paradigmatic of what can be called – if anything – 'collective self-identity'? How far can we study by means of this tradition how questionable particular forms of 'collective' identity or 'corporate identity' are, say when they are based on collective assimilation? It remains decisive for the formation of the self of communities not to assert any general phenomenon, not even right across 'the religions', but to note the distinctive logic of the different traditions; otherwise the differentiated forms of the formation of a self of communities would be concealed in the very approach to it.

What does it mean to become and to be a 'self'?

To keep to the urgent question posed by talk of identity: what does it mean under the conditions of growing anonymity and pluralization mentioned above to be and to become a 'self'? The question is *not* focussed on a self which is asserted only as an individual self and thus is already formalized, which in its own expression still ultimately remains anonymous, and is not articulated. In that case the demand to respect people in their individuality and self-determination paradoxically continues the process of making anonymous which leaves people the same, and isolated. So everything depends on how it is possible to gain a self which does not disappear in the black box of an individual 'I am' that is only generally asserted and its self-determination, but which is present as a self for others and itself without simply being 'identified' by others or even by itself (through an image of the self).[3]

How is it possible to become or to be a *self* and at the same time to be a self for others and with others? Only in this tense and inseparable form can identity be described as becoming a self and then be opposed to those processes of pluralization and increasing anonymity on which the critical remembrance of human identity focusses.

'Becoming a self' in the Christian tradition

The critical indications of the loss of the formation of identity are in a special way a reference to Christian traditions, because in them 'becoming a self' is manifestly the cornerstone of talk about human beings. Following its biblical origin, the Christian tradition speaks of human beings as those who are constantly chosen anew by God as his creatures, both as individuals and in community. In becoming what they are, these human beings are put in a history, brought up, changed. In its logic shaped by the Bible the Christian tradition sees human being as in the process of becoming. Here 'becoming' does not mean development but being created, being saved and being transformed. The history of this becoming can be understood and narrated only as the history of God, the creator and redeemer. This becoming is a dramatic becoming, which takes up and reflects on the brokenness of human development. Biblical and Christian talk of the becoming human of human beings thus maintains, as a central tendency, that the whole drama of human existence is part of 'becoming a self'. This contradicts the view that human beings are only either determined (say by their nature) or exposed to any kind of shaping and influence. Such an alternative brackets out that history which human beings do not bring upon themselves, but which they experience as the history of their becoming. Human beings become a self through the story of what they experience in their own actions.[3] Not everything is part of this story. It is not the history of these or those events which lends itself to becoming a self but what makes human beings share in the history which God enters into with them. That gives rise to a story which is not self-made, a story of *becoming* a self.[4]

In such a history groups of people also become a self, a family or a community; through this community they first gain the perspective of being a community. In it they find the possibility of speaking of themselves and of their history, or narrating it as a self. That is how the Christian tradition understands the history of the people of God, Israel, and that is how it understands the history of the Christian church. This gains its self only through the particular history in which it experiences God's action, not through a self-description or programmatic self-understanding. Both the individual's and the historical community's becoming a self belong together in the biblical tradition. The individual takes part in the story of the community and the community find its self in the history of each individual. It can then be asked critically of other identities which are given or somehow come into being what identity they assign to themselves or others.

The biblical origin of the Christian understanding of becoming a self [5]

In this respect the Christian tradition can reflect on its biblical origin. Thus in biblical discourse this form of becoming a self is maintained throughout, as is indicated clearly for the history of exegesis in Psalm 8. There it is said of human beings, 'What is man, that you, God, remember him?' The question is not 'What is "man"?' or 'What are his characteristics?' The question is asked, in wonder and praise, what this man is who has experienced this God as one who accepts him, as one who has begun on a history with him. Every individual human being will be able to repeat this time and again, 'Who am I, O God, that you think of me?' Anyone who asks this question immediately emerges from the anonymity of a determined natural being and similarly from the indeterminacy of a human existence which is given over solely to its own shaping or that of others. Those who reflect on the history of their becoming a self need not see their self dissolved between determinism and shaping their own lives, but can find it in what happens to them as human beings, addressed to them, according to God's will. 'Praise the Lord, O my soul, and do not forget the good things he has done for you' (Ps. 103.2). Here we have the words of someone who lives by the experiences which let him become a human being and in doing so gains his self. That is the good thing that befalls him.

The brokenness of the Christian traditions – in the context of the pluralization of religious culture? [6]

Because the Christian traditions have their focal point in this understanding of the human being and not in an abstract image of the human being or principle of personal dignity, they must be aware that they are challenged to oppose any attempts to deprive men and women of this characteristic of a self-identity. Therefore it will not be enough to counter this development with the demand for 'human beings' to be protected or preserved as persons with their 'individuality'. The question is how becoming a self emerges in its contours, even if under the current conditions of growing anonymity this happens in a broken way, which means not without the drama of becoming and being a person. However, for the Christian tradition this very drama is also part of becoming a self. Here the Christian tradition cannot be rela-tivized in reference to other religious identities. The point is that human beings are not put in the artificial situation of possibly seeking an identity in a wide-ranging religious offer, but may entrust themselves to the history of becoming a self which grows out of attention to God's creative action.

In that case the theme is not a general loss of tradition or a situation of competition between the religions and a loss of the formation of identity which is bound up with it; it is rather that of a new self which may keep finding itself anew in its very own history and which therefore cannot be preserved as something that is asserted in competition or handed down, even in the content of the *image* of a human being that needs to be maintained. It appears and is lived as a self. The perspective in which the theme of human identity put by the Christian tradition is not just the safeguarding of human identity or even self-assertion, but the continual possibility of becoming a self.

The presence of the self.

So to this degree it is all important that this becoming a self is made *present*, that it does not remain unarticulated,[7] but emerges to encounter others, not just as something that they have to note but also as a communication to them which they cannot experience otherwise and which can lead them to give up something of themselves in favour of another. So what is the significance of that which is special not only in respect of the other but also in respect of the other's becoming a self and then also in respect of the perception and experience of what can be called the 'good life'? To what extent does the 'good life' prove to be *becoming* a self, a life in the history of God, a life in 'sanctification', as the Christian tradition has called it?

Thus the issue is no longer the task of the liberal system of the law to protect the individual or communities in an identity which is fixed only formally, perhaps in their autonomy. Rather, the issue is the nature of the 'incorporation of the other',[8] so that this other is not only respected anony-mously but also gets a chance to express his or her make-up and experiences of identity and get a hearing. At *this* point the aspects of communitarian ethics[9] which focus on incorporating the other into understanding are important.[10] This understanding must be a communitarian one, since moral discourse based on particular rational arguments is inadequate. What is needed is a complex form of co-existence, of life together in justice. In that way it becomes possible for the special nature of individuals, what they experience, not to be taken up into a generality and be done away with, but to come into play as special factors without propagating an incalculable demand to do justice to the other.[11] It should become evident that each person experiences something more from the special nature of the individual or the community, indeed is shown how human life can *become good,* an experience which can be had only from the other, only from the other who becomes a self.

   This once again raises the key question, which has already been implicitly presupposed, of what constitutes the special nature of the individual and why a corresponding ethic is needed for *this* to come into play. To be more precise, there are two questions: first, what is the focus of the moral-philosophical or moral-theological interest if it investigates individuals not just in their special character which is postulated formally, and secondly, how – by the criterion of this question – this special character is to be understood. This second question can be understood as the quest for the 'principle of individuation'. However, that fixes it as a principle and not perhaps as a development which is very different for individuals, in which the important thing is this difference, in other words in which that the individuation appears as the becoming of a self. But reflection in moral theology and moral philosophy has after all kept attempting to define this principle which makes the individual an individual, and it can in no way leave it at a general demand for respect or even just 'tolerance' of the individual. Rather, it has sought in various ways to know how individuals coms into play with what constitutes them and how far then these individuals, these selves, are to be had as those who require not only to be noted in discourse but also to commit to the singular history of which they are the starting point.

The theological understanding of becoming a self

Thus philosophical and theological ethics has taken note of the fact that the special character of the individual cannot be given by chance, in the sense that others identify it. Theological reflection in ethics has noted that the special character of the individuals has to be recognized as something original, as selves which live from certain sources and want to be recognized in this originality, if the preservation of the identity of these selves is not to get stuck in their own accounts of themselves.[12] But to that degree this can be grasped only theologically, because the special nature of *becoming* a self cannot be constituted interpersonally.[13] Here the Other comes into play, who perceives and accepts individuals each in their peculiarity, without identifying them as it were from an alien aspect. Here we have to talk of the Other as the God who knows human beings[14] and in his righteousness gives them what they need. God's righteousness and goodness appear in God's history with human beings, not independently of them in an abstract faith.

However, to experience God's defining and transforming righteousness and goodness does not mean to leave behind all the given peculiarities of life; on the contrary, God's righteousness and goodness are present precisely in these realities and in relation to them. Thus in a particular situation, in a special encounter with another person, in a sickness, men and women can experience that they are not abandoned by God; they can experience God's care from another, perhaps quite new, aspect in the context of their history, and need not run the risk of losing their self because something has broken into their life which perhaps they cannot cope with or which they can understand only as a contradiction to their own self-determination. It is here that the specific peculiarity of individuals becomes evident: they do not discover themselves as 'cases' or 'examples', perhaps as the case of a sickness; each is a self who can speak of his or her experience as a self (in this sense) and may expect to be heard.

At this point there has been talk in the Christian tradition of the creative love of God, where human beings can say 'I' without needing always to reflect whether they have already long since become this or that for the Other. Accordingly, love of God means love of neighbour, encountering the other in such a way that this 'I' is not lost to the other. So one can say:

> What is Christian as distinct from other philosophical traditions begins and ends with the revelation that the infinite God loves the individual infinitely, and this is indicated most precisely in the fact that in human form he dies the death of the redeemer (i.e. of the sinner) for this beloved person. I do not become conscious of who 'I' am from a general 'know yourself' . . . but from the repercussion of the act of Christ who tells me at the same time how valuable I am to God and how lost I was before God . . . So my 'I' is God's Thou, and I can only be an 'I' because God wills to make himself my 'Thou'.[15]

This summary formulation by Hans Urs von Balthasar makes clear in what way the encounter of God as the Other with the individual is the whole subject of reflection here – and how only in this *whole drama* between God and human beings does it become possible to gain a self. The interlocking of the human encounter in the I and Thou with the (trinitarian) history between God and Jesus Christ is the presupposition for this reflection. Taken up by and transcended in this history, human beings remain pre-served from commandeering the Other and perceiving no more than what is created ever anew by God and thus loved. Because this Other encounters us in Christ, the Other can be who he is; he may remain in his special nature and need not prove himself to us in his humanity.

In this way the biblical talk of *righteousness* can be heard.[16] In this righteousness human beings are known[17] as those who they should may and appear, and not as those who are seen and identified. To practise this righteousness is a fundamental activity in which human beings come into play in their special nature, not as cases or as anonymous counterparts. In this righteousness the Other first appears as the Thou who communicates himself. However – as in any christological reflection – things do not stop at an exclusive relationship of I and Thou which excludes any others; a third party always comes into play, in that the I and the Thou encounter each other as those who share their history with God. They may always rely on this history; they are already part of it by right. Respect for their rights is not fundamentally endangered, and the situation of a constant safeguarding of individual rights to protection does not arise. The right of the other is an inseparable part of the structure of an ethic which aims at incorporating the other in the right way and not by surrendering the history of their identity along with the specific righteousness which they share in by virtue of their special nature, and the special nature which they seek not only to respect abstractly but also to understand. This is reflected in many ways in Christian tradition and teaching.

The vulnerability and the critical power of becoming a self

There is a particular fragility and vulnerability about becoming a self; it does not consist in firm relationships, as if it were always given, but in the dramatic events of creaturely life as described by the Christian tradition. This perception has its specific critical force in the face of the manifold phe-nomena where stories do not turn out right, in the face of the commandeer-ing of the other, in the face of questionable mechanisms of manipulation, assimilation or even recognition.

If becoming a self, with all its drama, is kept in view, then the manifold phenomenon of the disappearance of particular forms of 'religious socializa-tion' or becoming a self and the formation of identity need not lead us astray into demanding such forms and in this way turning the formation of identity into a programme. Far less can the consequence be to enter into a competition of identities. This could conflict with identity as becoming a self. Christian churches cannot therefore want to offer competitive identities, perhaps corporate identities, perhaps the identity of religious communities in the competition of religions or confessions.[18] If they did that, they would nonsensically give up what becoming a self uniquely means in the Christian context. However, they can oppose the prevention and the loss of identity-forming by contradicting the logic of appropriation and dispossession, of profiling and recognition. In the Christian tradition, becoming a self means being allowed to enter the history in which one may be *someone*, not for any other or against another, or even for a purpose, but as someone who is not robbed for this form of creaturely life, i.e. becoming a self. When people are compelled to assert themselves and stand out competitively, this form of Christian identity with its sharp contours is lost. The form will show itself all the more in its own recalcitrance when the laws of competition and competence also dominate life together in the church. More demands are made of Christian faith over the presence of this creaturely form of life than in any other respect. It uniquely preserves the experience that human life assumes its form by not closing itself to its history with God, which is the history of God's righteousness.

Translated by John Bowden

Notes

1. Cf. *Identität und Verständigung, Standort und Perspektiven des Religionsunterrichts in der Pluralität. Eine Denkschrift der Evangelischen Kirche in Deutschland*, Gütersloh 1994.

2. Paul Ricoeur has developed this distinction between idem-identity and ipse-identity. I largely follow this distinction. This is fundamental to the understanding of identity. Cf. P. Ricoeur, *Oneself as Another*, Chicago 1992.

3. For the development of this insight also as the foundation of ethics as an experiential ethic grounded in experience see Dietmar Mieth, *Moral und Erfahrung* II, *Entfaltung einer theologisch-ethischen Hermeneutik*, Freiburg, etc. 1998.

4. For further development see the discussion on narrative theology and story theology. See also Dietrich Ritschl, *The Logic of Theology*, London 1986. For further discussion see Stanley Hauerwas and L.Gregory Jones (eds), *Why Narrative? Readings in Narrative Theology*, Grand Rapids 1989.

5. For the exegetical-hermeneutical discussion and explanation see Adele

Reinhartz, '*Why ask My Name?' Anonymity and Identity in Biblical Narrative*, Oxford 1998.

6. Cf. Hans Waldenfels, 'Zur gebrochenen Identität des abendländischen Christentums', in *Religion und Identität. Im Horizont des Pluralismus*, ed. Werner Gephardt and Hans Waldenfels, Frankfurt 1999, 105–24.

7. This is the focus of Charles Taylor's characterization of the self in its presence: *Sources of the Self: The Making of the Modern Identity*, Cambridge 1989.

8. Cf. Jürgen Habermas, *Die Einbeziehung des Anderen. Studien zur politischen Theorie*, Frankfurt am Main ²1997.

9. For a discussion see Axel Honneth (ed.), *Kommunitarismus. Eine Debatte über die moralischen Grundlagen moderne Gesellschaften*, Frankfurt am Main and New York 1993, and some contributions in more recent theological discussion: Edmund Arens, 'Kirchlicher Kommunitarismus', *Theologische Revue* 94, 1998, 488–500.

10. This and not another foundation model is decisive in the contribution of communitarian ethics to ethic theory.

11. For this question see Hans J. Schneider, 'Das Allgemeine als Zufluchtsort. Eine kritische Anmerkung zur Diskursethik', in *Zwischen Universalismus und Relativismus*, ed. Horst Steinmann and Andreas G. Scherer, Frankfurt 1998, 179–90.

12. See the account of the history of moral philosophy in Taylor, *Sources of the Self* (n.7).

13. For the question see Walter Sparn (ed.), *Wer schreibt meine Lebensgeschichte? Biographie, Autobiographie, Hagiographie und ihre Enstehungszusammenhänge*, Gütersloh 1990.

14. Cf. Psalm 1.6.

15. Hans Urs von Balthasar.

16. Emmanuel Lévinas has rediscovered this phenomenon in its biblical structure; cf. especially E. Lévinas, 'Der Anderer, die Utopie und die Gerechtgikeit', in id., *Zwischen uns. Versuch über das Denken an den Anderen*, Munich and Vienna 1995, 165–78. For the biblical tradition cf. above all Gerhard von Rad, *Old Testament Theology I, The Theology of the Historical Traditions of Israel*, London 1975, 382–95: Yahweh's and Israel's righteousness. Cf. Hans G. Ulrich, 'Erfahren in Gerechtigkeit. Über das Zusammentreffen von Rechtfertigung und Recht', in *Rechtfertigung und Erfahrung. Gerhard Sauter zum 60. Geburtstage*, ed. M. Beintker, E. Mauer, H. Stoevesandt and H. G. Ulrich, Gütersloh 1995, 362–84.

17. Cf. Psalm 1.6: God 'knows' the way of the righteous.

18. This distinction has been noted in the memorandum *Identität und Verständigung* (n.1).

DOCUMENTATION

How *Concilium* Began

PAUL BRAND

To celebrate thirty-five years of its existence, Concilium *held its annual meeting during the week of Pentecost 1999 in Rome. The meeting was opened on 25 May with a press conference in the Casa Pro Unione. This was the large library room with a view on the Piazza Navona in which* Concilium *was first presented to the public in 1964, during the Second Vatican Council. On 26 May a public collo-quium was held in the Casa Internationale del Clero based on* Unanswered Questions *(the title of* Concilium *1999/1). As every year, the next two days were devoted to the annual business (personal matters, evaluation of the previous year's issues and the planning of new numbers). On 29 May, at the concluding gathering, Paul Brandt gave a short speech. This year, though, it had a special character. Paul knew that it would be his last speech. A publisher by profession, Paul Brandt is not only one of the founders of* Concilium, *but had also previously spent years developing the plan of such a journal when others felt this impossible. He remained loyal to his journal for thirty-five years. He worked continuously on the Foundation, did not miss a single conference and along with the directors of* Concilium *developed many personal contacts.*

On 1 January 2000 Paul Brand and Ton van den Boogaard, for thirty-five years the President of Concilium, *resigned.* Concilium *owes a great deal to both these men. As a means of documenting this noteworthy change, here we present the speech given by Paul Brand, since in its simplicity it has preserved something of the original living spirit in which* Concilium *came into being at the time of the Second Vatican Council.*

I was a publisher in the Netherlands. In part I published theology, in part other books. I came into contact with Dutch theologians, but more with French and German theologians who – by the standards of the time – were regarded as progressive. Because I was very attracted by their thought, I felt that they should also be published in the Netherlands. And because I believe that a publisher cannot publish the book of an author with whom he has no personal contact, at the beginning of the 1950s I began to visit above all

German-speaking authors. I had intensive contact with Romano Guardini and Karl Rahner, and later with Hans Küng, Hans Urs von Balthasar, Johann Baptist Metz, Walter Kasper and Joseph Ratzinger, and in France with Yves Congar and M.-D.Chenu. As a non-theologian I found some of their books particularly hard to read; but through regular personal contact with the authors I got to know them better. I put my questions and expressed my personal views, and this led to a series of private lectures and at the same time to a deep bond. Rahner and Küng visited the Netherlands, gave lectures, and stayed either with me or in the manse at Ankeveen, the village in which I live. I followed their scholarly work as far as I could, and made my modest contribution by asking the theologians, after the many conversations, to write on particular topics, in the form of either articles or meditations. Now I felt that I was being a real publisher.

In this atmosphere, in 1958 I asked Karl Rahner to join me in founding an international Catholic scholarly journal for theology. I had sketched out a first plan for it. But despite our long conversations and my urgent request Rahner decided against it. 'We cannot write what we would like to write,' he said.

In November 1962, during the first session of the Second Vatican Council, the schema *De Fontibus Revelationis*, a working paper by conservative Vatican theologians under the leadership of Cardinal Ottaviani and Sebastiaan Tromp SJ, was rejected by almost two-thirds of the bishops. A day later Pope John XXIII withdrew this schema. That evening I again went to Rahner (he was living in the Gregoriana) and asked him a second time to found an international scholarly theological journal. After a long conversation he agreed and asked me to work out a draft. The next morning I visited Hans Küng (who was living in Rome in the villa of the bishop of Rottenburg). He joined us. In the afternoon I went to Edward Schillebeeckx in the Dutch College, and he too agreed to collaborate. The long years of patient waiting had borne fruit, and I returned to the Netherlands content, to work out the plans. On 12 January 1963 I again spoke with Rahner, who was spending some days in Cologne, and we resolved to appoint a secretary for further organization and to implement the plan, for the other activities of my publishing house had to go on. With the help of Schillebeeckx and his Flemish provincial I was able to persuade Fr Van Hengel OP to take over the function of secretary. In June 1963 we discussed the plans for two days in Saarbrücken with around twenty theologians. We arrived at a so-called *constituante* and resolved to begin work.

During the years in which the Second Vatican Council was taking place in

Rome (1962–1965) we rented a couple of rooms in a small hotel there in which I established the secretariat. Not only were all the bishops and so-called *periti*, but also the personal advisers of the bishops and the best Catholic theologians in the world, in Rome at that time. So they were reachable. I visited above all the theologians and Van Hengel made contact with the bishops. In circular letters he regularly reported the latest developments over the journal. Proofs were sent out and put in the post-boxes of the bishops on St Peter's Square. Thus bishops from all over the world were informed of our activities.

At the request of the theologians directly involved, the journal, which we called *Concilium*, was put in an independent foundation. With much support from Ton van den Boogaard, a Nijmegen businessman, who was very interested in the plan, and from Rahner, Küng, Congar and Schillebeeckx, in 1965 the journal appeared in nine, later in seven, languages. That took a good deal of time, money and work. Ten numbers each of around 50,0000 words appeared in the first five years. The ten numbers were also distributed over ten theological disciplines: dogmatics, pastoral theology, moral theology, spirituality, exegesis, church history, canon law, church and world (fundamental theology), liturgy and ecumenical theology. For each number we looked for, and found, two main editors; there were a further ten advisory theologians for the whole project.

Different meetings took place each year over the period when they were all living in Rome. All these (at that time male) theologians with their great variety of dress formed a colourful and attractive group. Later we assessed the issues that had appeared and agreed on the topics of the issues that were to appear two years later. An issue was not just a pot-pourri of articles; each discussed a specific theme – as it still does today.

After the end of Vatican II we met once a year, each time in a different part of the world. When there were financial difficulties, the question was discussed whether we should not hold meetings every two years instead of every years. I opposed the proposal, since I believe that theologians should not only read one another but should meet regularly. Personal conversations and discussions between them, and the international character of such encounters, are very important for the development of theological thought. In this way the division between German, Roman and French theology and that in other languages was overcome, and gave place to an undivided theology. Without exception there was deep trust between the participants, and world-wide friendships developed.

At the beginning the Jesuits thought that too many Dominicans were involved, and the Dominicans thought that there were too many Jesuits; yet others thought that the number of Germans and French was disproportionately great. We had to attempt to achieve a proportionate distribution all over the world. That gave rise to vigorous, but interesting, conversations. Nor was there a single language for discussions. Each spoke his own language – French, German or English. In the first years Rahner even spoke Latin. When there were problems of understanding, a member of the session translated.

Of course there were also tensions. The Vatican was not happy about the *Concilium* project and thought that a Roman theologian should have been appointed a member. Mgr Carlo Colombo, the house theologian of Paul VI, was envisaged. So in the sessions before the appearance of the first number there was often discussion of the question: what is more important, the hierarchy or theology? The theologians thought that they had to have the freedom to say what they wanted to say, but Colombo thought that the Curia must have the last word. He thought that for each number a couple of bishops should be appointed as censors. But he was opposed by Rahner, Mgr Edelby and Congar, and could not carry the day with his proposal.

Colombo sometimes introduced a matter with the words, 'From higher authority I must say . . .' That amounted to saying, 'The pope thinks . . .' Once he invited Rahner, Schillebeeckx and me to the Café San Pietro, near St Peter's, for a conversation. He declared: 'From higher authority, I must say that the appointment of Hans Küng as chief editor for the issue on ecumenical theology is impossible.' When he noted that we did not share his view he proposed: 'Perhaps Küng can become deputy chief editor.' We did not accept that, nor did we agree to a further proposal. Colombo went away, and although he had invited us, he let me pay.

We also had problems with Jean Daniélou, not at that time a cardinal. Daniélou had told me several times that he was against *Concilium*, since this journal damaged the power of the Curia. He made sure that French Jesuits might not take part in it (H.de Lubac had to resign), nor could the English Dominicans. Daniélou became a cardinal in 1969, Rahner did not. Congar become a cardinal only much later, at a great old age. Anyone who took an active part in *Concilium* certainly did not attain this honour.

Over his long years as President of the Foundation, Ton van den Boogaard still kept attempting to get on good terms with the church, but I constantly told him that this was a lost labour of love. 'They are friendly towards you, but when it comes to the point, they drop you.' Moreover a kind of counterpart to *Concilium* was created, *Communio*, which finally

Ratzinger and von Balthasar joined. But despite the sometimes great pressure and despite great tensions we have succeeded in continuing and maintaining our independence. That's a bit of history. Before I close, let me add a few wishes for the future.

Readability

My first wish relates to the readability of *Concilium*. Every year now we say how difficult this journal is to read. You, the theologians, write about theology as a learned discipline, and that is how it must remain. But it is also very important for you to write as readably as possible, for this discipline is more than mathematics or chemistry. Theology is about people, God, love, life and death. That is why theology is so important.

While you are writing, you (and all the authors whom you get to work with you) must think of all the people who are working, day in and day out, at the grass roots of the church and society, who must draw inspiration from you and then hand it on. At present I often find your texts very difficult to read because you write in such an academic way. Even I have trouble reading them. You should stop producing footnotes half a page or a page long. We are well aware that you are experts in your discipline; you needn't show that in every article. You must be clear that what you write must also be a help to simple priests and colleagues in pastoral work who are working in difficult circumstances in Asia, North and South America, Africa and Europe. You must support them. So you must see that readable articles appear in *Concilium*, including meditative texts and articles on topical themes.

That brings me to another wish.

Topicality

Today many Catholics worry about the commandments and prohibitions of the church. For example, many women were raped in Kosovo. International organizations made great efforts to brings as many 'morning after' pills as possible to Kosovo. Thereupon the *Osservatore Romano* accused these organizations of murder. You must oppose this. Then the Dutch cardinal appeared on television and stated that first of all one must understand such action with the pill, but if one thought about it carefully one would also recognize that suffering was an essential element of Christianity. I think that that is a scandal. As if the degree to which a people suffers elevates the status of their Christianity! Suffering is an affliction which we must seek to overcome. The church is there to bring people happiness. It must make them strong in love and solidarity.

Another example: divorced people may not come to communion. Everyone knows that a divorce is a particularly painful and grievous matter for all concerned: but instead of helping them, the church gives them one more kick. By contrast, a dictator like Pinochet, who is responsible for the death, disappearance and torture of thousands of people, receives communion every morning, once even at the pope's hands. What are we to make of that?

And there are many more topical questions: homosexuality, the pill, condoms in the fight against Aids, birth control, celibacy, women's ministry, abortion, euthanasia: you must write, legibly and clearly, about all these things. Those are some wishes for the future.

Finally I want to thank some individuals. I begin with special thanks to Ton van der Boogaard, who for thirty years has been working for the finances; he did so particularly successfully during the difficult 1980s. Thanks, too, for those who worked on the colloquium of the past week and thanks to those who chaired the press conference and the annual meeting. That wasn't easy.

Thanks too to the directors who retire this year, and also to the directors from former years who have come on the occasion of our thirty-fifth anniversary celebration, Luis Maldonado and Knut Walf, David Tracy, who has brought together Western European and North American theology, and Virgil Elizondo for his efforts working with the church of South America. He made sure that Gustavo Gutiérrez and Leonardo Boff took part; he also made contact with Helder Camara and Oscar Beozzo. When I see him or read him, I also think of the word pastoral. This afternoon I telephoned Bas van Iersel, who since 1964 has been part of *Concilium* and very active in it, but now is gravely ill. He sent his warmest greetings.

And finally, thanks to all our publishers, who work so hard for *Concilium*. I wish God's blessing on all of us personally and on *Concilium*.

Paul Brandt

Contributors

DIETMAR MIETH was born in 1940 and studied theology, German and philosophy. He gained his doctorate in theology at Würzburg in 1968 and his Habilitation in theological ethics in Tübingen in 1974. He became Professor of Moral Theology in Fribourg, Switzerland in 1974 and Professor of Theological Ethics in Tübingen in 1981. His publications include *Die Einheit von vita activa und vita contemplativa*, Regensburg 1969; *Dichtung, Glaube und Moral*, Mainz 1976; *Epik und Ethik*, Tübingen 1976; *Moral und Erfahrung*, Fribourg CH ³1983; *Meister Eckhart* (which he edited), Munich ³1986; *Gotteserfahrung – Weltverantwortung*, Munich 1982; *Die neuen Tugenden*, Düsseldorf 1984; *Geburtenregelung*, Mainz 1990; *Schwangerschaftsabbruch*, Freiburg im Breisgau 1991; *Das gläserne Glück der Liebe*, Freiburg im Breisgau 1992; *Grundbegriffe der christlichen Ethik*, Paderborn 1992 (with J. P. Wils); *Religiose Erfahrung, Historische Modelle in christlicher Tradition*, Munich 1992, which he edited with W. Haug; and *Moraltheologie im Abseits, Antwort auf die Enzyklika 'Veritatis Splendor'*, Freiburg im Breisgau ²1995, which he edited.

Address: Universität Tübingen Katholisch-Theologisches Seminar, Liebermeisterstrasse 12, 72076 Tübingen, Germany.

ALBERT W. MUSSCHENGA was born in 1950. As well as being director of the *Bezinningscentrum* of the Free University of Amsterdam, he is Professor of Social Ethics in the Department of Philosophy of the Free University. He is founder and former head of the university's Institute of Ethics and currently the director of the Netherlands School for Research in Practical Philosophy. The Dutch organization for scientific research NWO commissioned him to develop a national research programme about 'Ethics and Public Policy'. He is co-editor of some scientific series.

Address and list of publications: aw.musschenga@dienst.vu.nl.

FELIX WILFRED was born in Tamilnadu, India in 1948. He is professor in the School of Philosophy and Religious Thought, State University of Madras, India. He has taught, as visiting professor, in the universities of Nijmegen, Münster, Frankfurt am Main and Ateneo de Manila. He was also a member of the International Theological Commission of the Vatican. He has been president of the Indian Theological Association, and Secretary of the Theological Commission of FABC. His researches and field-studies today cut across many disciplines in humanities and social sciences. Among his publications in the field of theology are: *From the Dusty Soil. Reinterpretation of Christianity* (1995); *Beyond Setled Foundations. The Journey of Indian Theology* (1993); *Sunset in the East? Asian Challanges and Christian Involvement* (1991); *Leave the Temple* (1992).

Address: University of Madras, Dept of Christian Studies, Chepauk, Madras, India.

ANNETTE KLEINFELD studied philosophy, German and the theatre in Karlsruhe and Münich. She has worked in human resource management, business culture development and corporate identity for an advisory firm in Munich. She has also specialized in the philosophy of economics and practical business ethics and gained a doctorate in this field at the University of Munich. She has also been academic assistant at the Philosophical Research Centre for Ethical, Economic and Business Culture in Hanover. She is currently a partner in an advisory firm on corporate ethics and value management in Hanover.

THOMAS GIL studied philosophy, social sciences and theology in Bonn and Münster, gaining his doctorate in 1981 and his habilitation in 1992; from 1989 to 1995 he lectured in the University of Stuttgart, and from 1993 to 1994 he was a visiting professor at the State University of New York; from 1995 to 1998 he was professor at the University of St Gallen and since 1998 he has been Professor of Practical Philosophy at the Technical University of Berlin; from 1996 he has also been Chaim Perelman Professor at the Free University of Brussels. His books include: *Ethik* (1993); *Gestalten des Utopischen. Zur Sozialpragmatik kollektiver Vorstellungen* (1997); *Sozialphilosophie der Arbeit* (1997); *Einführung in philosophisches Denken. Erfahrung, Reflexion, Urteil, Handeln* (1998); *Demokratische Technikbewertung* (1999);

Contributors

139

Kritik der klassischen Geschichtsphilosophie (1999); he has also written articles on questions of practical philosophy, ethics, social philosophy, the philosophy of law and the philosophy of technology.

Address: Rönnestrasse 5, 14057 Berlin, Germany.

JAMES F. KEENAN, SJ, is Professor of Moral Theology at the Weston Jesuit School of Theology and chair of the Catholic Theological Coalition on HIV/AIDS Prevention. He received his STL and STD from the Gregorian University. Books include *Goodness and Rightness in Thomas Aquinas' Summa Theologiae* (1992); *Virtues for Ordinary Christians* (1996) and *Commandments of Compassion* (1999). He has edited *The Context of Casuistry* (1995); *Practice What You Preach: Virtues, Ethics and Power in the Lives of Pastoral Ministers and Their Congregations* (1999) and *HIV/AIDS Prevention: Catholic Moral Theologians Explore Cases Globally* (1999). His articles have appeared in many journals.

LUIZ CARLOS SUSIN was born in Caixas do Sul in Brazil in 1949. A Capuchin friar since 1968, he holds a degree in philosophy and a doctorate in theology from the Gregorian University in Rome. He teaches systematic theology at the Pontifical Catholic University of Rio Grande do Sul and the Franciscan Higher School of Theology and Spirituality in Porto Alegre, is a visiting lecturer to the Latin American Confederation of Bishops in Bogotá and the Antonianum in Rome, and is currently President of the Brazilian Society for Theology and Religious Studies. His published works include *O homem messiânico* (an introduction to the thought of Emmanuel Lévinas, 1983), *Moral emergente* (1989), *Assim na terra como no céu* (1995) and *Jesus, Filho de Deus e Filho de Maria* (1997), as well as articles in the fields of faith and culture.

Address: Faculté de Théologie PUCRS, Avenue Ipirauga 6681, 90619–900 Porto Alegre (RS), Brazil.

AGUSTÍN DEL AGUA was born in 1947 and holds a licentiate in biblical sciences from the Biblical Institute in Rome and a doctorate of theology from the Comillas Pontifical University of Madrid as well as a doctorate in trilingual biblical philology from the Complutensian University of Madrid. He lectures and pursues research at the San Pablo University of Madrid. His publications include *Evangelizar el Reino de Dios. Estudio redaccional del concepto lucano de Basileia* (1984) and *El método midrásico y la exégesis del Nuevo Testamento* (1985). He is editor and co-author of *Antropología y Humanismo* (1999) and co-author of *Personajes del Antiguo Testamento* I (1998).

Address: Conferencia Episcopal Española, Añastro 1, Madrid 28033, Spain.

HERMANN HÄRING was born in 1937 and studied theology in Munich and Tübingen; between 1969 and 1980 he worked at the Institute of Ecumenical Research in Tübingen; since 1980 he has been Professor of Dogmatic Theology at the Catholic University of Nijmegen. His books include *Kirche und Kerygma. Das Kirchenbild in der Bultmannschule*, 1972; *Die Macht des Bösen. Das Erbe Augustins*, 1979; *Zum Problem des Bösen in der Theologie*, 1985; *Hans Küng. Breaking Through*, London 1998; *Das Böse in der Welt*, 1999. He was co-editor of the *Wörterbuch des Christentums*, 1988, and has written articles on ecclesiology and christology, notably in the *Tijdschrift voor Theologie*.

Address: Katholieke Universiteit, Faculteit der Godgeleerdheit, Erasmusgebouw, Erasmusplein I, 6525 HT Nijmegen, Netherlands.

CHRISTINE FIRER HINZE is Associate Professor of Christian Ethics at Marquette University. She received a PhD from the University of Chicago Divinity School in 1989, and her BA and MA in theology from the Catholic University of America. Her research and writing focusses on foundational issues in Christian social ethics, including understandings of power and social transformation; Catholic social thought; and economic and social questions concerning women, work, and families. Her articles have appeared in many journals; she is the author of *Comprehending Power in Christian Social Ethics* (1995) and *Making a Living* (forthcoming).

Address: Department of Theology, Room 100 Coughlin Hall, Marquette University, PO Box 1881, Milwaukee, WI 53225, USA.

HANS G. ULRICH was born in Stettin in 1942 and studied Protestant theology and social sciences in Heidelberg and Göttingen. He gained his

doctorate in Mainz and his habilitation in Bonn. He has taught in Bonn,
Houston and Athens and since 1982 has been Professor of Systematic
Theology and Ethics at the theological faculty of Erlangen-Nuremberg. His
books include: *Anthropologie und Ethik bei Friedrich Nietzsche* (1975);
Eschatologie und Ethik (1988); *Freiheit im Leben mit Gott. Texte zur Tradition
evangelischer Ethik* (1990). He has written articles on the theory of theological ethics, ethics in English, social ethics, business ethics and bioethics.

Address: Coburgerstrasse 49a, 90156 Erlangen, Germany.

CONCILIUM

Concilium: Subscription Information

Issues to be published in 2000

February   2000/1: *Evolution and Faith*
edited by Hermann Häring and Christoph Theobald

April   2000/2: *Creating Identity*
edited by Hermann Häring, Maureen Junker-Kenny and Dietmar Mieth

June   2000/3: *Religion During and After Communism*
edited by Miklós Tomka and Paul M. Zulehner

October   2000/4: *The Bright Side of Faith*
edited by Elsa Tamez and Ellen van Wolde

December   2000/5: *In the Power of Wisdom*
edited by Maria Pilar Aquino and Elisabeth Schüssler Fiorenza

----

To receive *Concilium 2000* (five issues) **anywhere in the world**, please copy this form, complete it in block capitals and send it with your payment to:

SCM Press *(Concilium)* 9–17 St Albans Place London N1 0NX England
Telephone (44) 20 7359 8033 Fax (44) 20 7359 0049

☐ Individual   **£25.00**/*US$50.00*   ☐ Institutional   **£35.00**/*US$75.00*

Issues are sent by air to the USA; please add £10/US$20 for airmail dispatch to all other countries (outside Europe).

☐ I enclose a cheque payable to SCM–Canterbury Press Ltd for £/$ ....

☐ Please charge my MasterCard/Visa   Expires...

........................../.............................../.............................../...............................

Signature ....

Name/Institution ....

Address ....

....

....

Telephone ....Fax ....

E-mail...